DAVID:

His Life and Psalms

DAVID:

His Life and Psalms

Jim Jordon

Gospel Advocate Co.
P.O. Box 150
Nashville, Tennessee 37202

Published by Gospel Advocate Co.
P.O. Box 150, Nashville, TN 37202

ISBN 0-89225-354-1

to my mother,
Mette Priscilla Jordon

PREFACE

This book has been a family project. My wife, Virginia, did the proofreading of the handwritten manuscript, correcting my spelling and grammar. My daughter, Mitzi Brown, did the copy editing and removed some of the archaic words I am prone to use. My son, Charles Kip Jordon, was responsible for the book being published. My mother and father, though not with us now, contributed long ago by instilling in me a love and deep reverence for God's Word.

I have written the book because I think David is worthy of more attention than he is given. His life offers counsel on many of today's pressing problems. Where else do we have an inspired narrative of one man's struggles, furnished with windows (his psalms) through which we can look into his soul and see his reaction to his struggles, his victories, and his secret sins? I have enjoyed the labor of writing and feel that I have been blessed by the study required. I hope the book may bring to readers a better understanding of God, of David, and of themselves. The glory is to the Lord for His love, patience, and grace.

Jim Jordon
February 1989

CONTENTS

CHAPTER 1

A Hero Worthy of Imitation

1 Samuel 16 through 18:7

Only one man in all the Bible wore the name *David*. He was a paradox in that he was both a national hero and an outlaw, a murderer and an angel of the Lord, a slayer of giants and a sensitive poet, a victorious king and a pleading penitent, an adulterer and a man who deeply loved and served God. He foreshadowed Christ, and Christ was called his son.

DAVID, THE SHADOW OF JESUS

The first verse of the New Testament reads, "The book of the generation of Jesus Christ, the son of David, the son of Abraham" (Matt. 1:1). Jesus was born in the city of David, was called the root of David, the seed of David, and was given the throne of David. And the New Testament closes with "I Jesus have sent mine angel to testify unto you these things in the churches. I am the root and the offspring of David, and the bright and morning star" (Rev. 22:16).[1]

Christ's relationship to David is stated even more clearly in Paul's opening address to the "men of

Israel" at Antioch in Pisidia. Paul, in introducing Jesus to them, went back to God's words concerning David. "I have found David the son of Jesse, a man after mine own heart, which shall fulfill all my will. Of this man's seed hath God, according to his promise, raised unto Israel a Savior, Jesus" (Acts 13:22, 23).

Therefore, does it not seem important that we as disciples of Christ know more of his progenitor, David, than that he slew the giant Goliath, committed adultery with Bathsheba, and authored many of the Psalms? Do we not need to know the characteristics of this man "who found favor before God" (Acts 7:46)? We are dealing with a man whose name is found six times in the first chapter of Matthew and more often (forty-three times) in the New Testament than any other Old Testament hero except Moses and Abraham.

DAVID'S BEGINNING

The story of David begins in 1 Samuel 16. He immediately becomes and remains the central figure for forty-two consecutive chapters of the Bible. Excluding Jesus, David is the leading character in more of God's Word than any man save Moses, and he by only three chapters.

David was born about 1085 B.C. in the village of Bethlehem. His great grandparents were Boaz and Ruth, of whom we read in that beautiful love story bearing her name. David's father was Jesse, but of his mother we know nothing. There is speculation concerning her character because of statements found in Psalms 51:5; 86:16; and 116:16, but we will deal with this matter later.

David was the youngest of Jesse's large family of sons and daughters. He had nephews who were close to his own age and who played much greater roles in his life than did his brothers. Watch for the names of Joab, Abishai, Asahel, and Amasa.

David's childhood days were spent in Bethlehem, a shepherd's village centrally located in the territory given to the tribe of Judah when the promised land was divided among the twelve tribes. Both David and Jesus were of the tribe of Judah, which fulfilled the prophecy of Father Israel when he said, "The scepter shall not depart from Judah" (Gen. 49:10). Both David and Jesus grew up to be kings and shepherds of God's people.

When first introduced in Scripture, David was a handsome man of about twenty with a dark, healthy complexion that came from an active outdoor life. He was powerfully built, yet gracefully quick in his actions. His personality was pleasant, and his speech was eloquent (1 Sam. 16:12, 18). As youngest brother, the lonely job of shepherding his father's flock of sheep had been passed down to him. One day as he was in the field with the sheep, someone came to relieve him, saying, "Your father wants to see you."

When he arrived at his house in Bethlehem, he was presented to Samuel, an already legendary character throughout Israel. Samuel had been God's spokesman and judge for so long that he was both feared and loved by great and small. He had scolded the people for wanting a king like other nations (1 Sam. 8:4-22), but he had finally hearkened to their request and anointed Saul, the son of Kish, as king (1 Sam. 10).

CHRONOLOGY OF DAVID

Place in Time (B.C.)	Place in His Life	PERIODS OF HIS LIFE	Place in the Scriptures	Psalms written
1085-65	0-20	CHILDHOOD Birth to Atonement	1 Samuel 16:13	0
1065-55	20-30	HERO—OUTLAW Goliath to Crowning	1 Samuel 16:13 to 2 Samuel 2:4	18
1055-35	30-50	VICTORIOUS KING Crowning to Sin with Bathsheba	2 Samuel 2:4–11:27 1 Chron. 11:1–20:3	22
1035-23	50-62	HARASSED KING Mid-life Crisis to Return to Jerusalem	2 Samuel 12:1–19:15	21
1023-1015	62-70	CONCLUDING YEARS Return to Jerusalem to Death	2 Samuel 19:16 to 1 Kings 2:11 1 Chron. 20:4–29:30	4
1085-15	70 years	OVERALL	1 Samuel 16:1 to 1 Kings 2:11 1 Chron. 11:1 to 29:30	85

Samuel was in Bethlehem to pass the spirit of God to a son of Jesus by anointing him to rule over God's chosen people. True, Saul was still very much alive. To God, however, he had died because of disobedience (1 Sam. 13:14; 15:22, 23; 16:14), and the throne was vacant. But Samuel was frightened of Saul and had protested when God first told him to go and anoint a new king. Nonetheless, he went.

Samuel was impressed with Jesse's oldest son, Eliab, but Jehovah passed him over because "the Lord seeth not as man seeth . . . for man looketh on the outward appearance, but the Lord looketh on the heart" (1 Sam. 16:7). When all the older sons had passed before Samuel and been rejected by God, the youngest was sent for, and David came before the Prophet. "Then Samuel took the horn of oil, and anointed him . . . and the Spirit of the Lord came upon David from that day forward" (1 Sam. 16:13). Therefore, we must remember when we read David's words that he was an inspired proclaimer (prophet) of the Lord (Matt. 22:43-45; Acts 2:25-31).

We are fortunate in studying this man chosen by God that we have not only the record of his outward actions but also the psalms that reveal his inner thoughts (Luke 6:45). Through these lyrical pictures of David's heart we can see why this very human man was so beloved of God.

DAVID AS A SHEPHERD

Before we become absorbed in the action-packed decade of David's life let's look at some of the characteristics developed by David in his formative years as he cared for his father's sheep. First, David developed a strong sense of responsibility and loyalty. He led his sheep to green pastures, he saw they had still waters from which to drink, and when "there came a lion, and a bear, and took a lamb out of the flock," he "went out after him, and smote him, and delivered it out of his mouth" (1 Sam. 17:34-35). David was not willing to compromise with a savage beast by sacrificing even one lamb to save the flock. Rather, he would willingly imperil himself to save the lamb. He was a good shepherd even as Christ said of Himself, "I am the good shepherd: the good shepherd giveth his life for the sheep" (John 10:11).

Second, David became an able antagonist. He was described early in his life as "a mighty valiant man, and a man of war" (1 Sam. 16:18). He had ample time to practice and use the sling, the rod, and the knife as he watched over the flock. Above all, he learned in times of conflict to place his trust in God. When he faced Goliath, he said, "The Lord that delivered me out of the paw of the lion, and out of the paw of the bear, he will deliver me out of the hand of this Philistine" (1 Sam. 17:37). This faith was also often demonstrated in David's psalms. He would begin to pray earnestly for the solution of a problem and then suddenly switch to praising God for the victory as if it had already occurred.

Third, David used his time to develop skill in music, which he used both to drive away evil (1 Sam. 16:23) and to praise the goodness of God. "My lips shall praise thee," he wrote (Psa. 63:3). In his early psalms, his most dominant theme was praise (in eleven out of seventeen psalms), and throughout his life he never ceased to praise God.

Later in his life he established the music of worship found in the Jewish religion.

Fourth, David's outdoor life led him to be filled with awe at the constant wonders of God's power and compassion. In Psalm 104, one of his earliest psalms, he described how Jehovah made the earth and cares for all the creatures "small and great." He was so overwhelmed that he cried out, "O Lord, how manifold are thy works! In wisdom hast thou made them all: the earth is full of thy riches" (v. 24). What vivid insight into the nature of God for the young shepherd to see that his God walked upon the wings of the wind and made the clouds chariots (v. 3). Notice how David both began and ended the psalm with the note of personal dedication, "Bless the Lord, O my soul."

Later, as a mature king, David wrote Psalm 19 with the same awe at the power of God. The imagery is more sophisticated, and God's written revelation awed him as much as the wonders of His natural creation, but the psalm ends with the simple prayer, "Let the words of my mouth, and the meditation of my heart, be acceptable in thy sight, O Lord, my strength, and my redeemer" (v. 14).

Still later, in Psalm 139, one of his last psalms, David continued to stand in awe of God's knowledge and cried out, "Such knowledge is too wonderful for me; it is high, I cannot attain unto it. . . . How precious also are thy thoughts unto me, O God! How great is the sum of them!" (vv. 6, 17). Here in old age the supplicant's prayer remained, "Search me, O God, and know my heart: . . . see if there be any wicked way in me, and lead me in the way everlasting" (vv. 23-24).

David never lost his childlike wonder at God's greatness as seen on every side and in everything. It kept him humble. He asked, "What is man, that thou art mindful of him?" (Psa. 8:4). Many today have ceased to stand amazed, and to these Christ said, "Except ye ... become as little children, ye shall not enter into the kingdom of heaven" (Matt. 18:3).

Fifth, along with the amazement of God's power and care, David also came to understand God's ever-present closeness to him as an individual. He wrote, "Whither shall I flee from thy presence? If I ascend up into heaven, thou art there: if I make my bed in hell behold, thou art there. If I take the wings of the morning, and dwell in the uttermost parts of the sea; even there shall thy hand lead me, and thy right hand shall hold me" (Psa. 139:7-10). This knowledge of the constant presence of an all-powerful, caring God gave David an undying assurance and optimism.

Thus, as a shepherd David was trained to be physically strong, mentally alert, and spiritually humble. Early in his life, David wrote the psalm of the shepherd, Psalm 23. How much it must have meant to him to have the Lord as his shepherd, and how much it can mean to us to know that Jesus is our shepherd! David might personalize it for us as follows: "Jesus is my shepherd; I shall not want. Jesus makes me to lie down in green pastures; Jesus leads me beside the still waters. Jesus restores my soul; Jesus leads me in paths of righteousness for His name's sake. Yea, though I walk through the valley of the shadow of death, I will fear no evil; for Jesus is with me; His rod and His staff, they comfort me. Jesus prepares a table before me in the presence of my enemies; Jesus anoints my head with oil; my cup runs over. Surely goodness and mercy shall follow me all the days of my life, and I will dwell in the house of Jesus forever."[2]

DAVID BECOMES THE NATIONAL HERO

During the later part of David's shepherding days, he was periodically called upon to play the harp for King Saul. The king was subject to fits of depression brought on by the evil spirit that had entered him when God's spirit had left (1 Sam. 16:14). The sweet music played by David refreshed Saul when he was in an evil mood. Thus David was busy going "back and forth from Saul to tend his father's sheep at Bethlehem" (1 Sam. 17:15, NIV).

For thirty years, Saul had reigned and not found peace. In fact, he "fought against all his enemies on every side. . . . And there was sore war against the Philistines all the days of Saul" (1 Sam. 14:47, 52). Saul's eldest son, Jonathan, had developed into a valiant soldier and was fighting at his side when the "Philistines gathered together their armies to battle . . . at Shochoh and Azekah" (1 Sam. 17:1). "Armies" was correct, because these migrants, as the name *Philistine* implies, formed a loose confederation of city-states in the southwest section of the land God had promised to His people. The lord of each city had his own army, but they were held together through their common ancestry to Mizraim, the son of Ham, the son of Noah (Gen. 10:6-14), and their common hatred of the Hebrews.

Saul moved his army to the east side of the valley of Elah, where it narrows to form a ravine called

Ephes-dammim, "the boundary of blood," so named because of the frequent battles that took place there. Separated by this ravine, the two armies encamped and studied each other. Each day a Philistine warrior named Goliath would shout across the narrow valley to the army of Israel, "Why are ye come out to set your battle in array? am not I a Philistine, and ye servants to Saul? choose you a man for you, and let him come down to me. If he be able to . . . kill me, then will we bė your servants: but if I . . . kill him, then shall ye be our servants" (1 Sam. 17:8-9).

Fear paralyzed Saul and the army of Israel. Saul, although he was head and shoulders taller than the average Israelite (1 Sam. 10:23), was no match physically for the Philistine. Goliath was a giant of a man from a family of giants (2 Sam. 21:18-22; 1 Chron. 20:5). He stood nine feet six inches tall, wore a protective coat of mail weighing 168 pounds, and carried a spear the head of which weighed 20 pounds.

Among those fearful Israelites were the three oldest brothers of David. After the brothers had been away for a month or more, it was natural for their father to wish to know what the news of battle was and to send a package of food to his sons. So Jesse asked David to go to the battle area to check on the three brothers. David "rose up early in the morning, and left the sheep with a keeper" (1 Sam. 17:20). He arrived at the battle scene just as "Israel and the Philistines had put the battle in array, army against army" (1 Sam. 17:21).

David heard Goliath's challenge and, feeling deeply the reproach to Israel, asked, "Who is this uncircumcised Philistine, that he should defy the armies of the living God?" (1 Sam. 17:26). Letting it be known that he would accept Goliath's challenge, David soon found himself standing before Saul, who pointed out that he was but a youth and thus was not able to go against the Philistine champion.

However, David *did* fight Goliath as the champion of the Israelites. What changed King Saul's mind about letting David go? It was David's assurance in Jehovah. Confidence breeds confidence. He told Saul how he had killed both a bear and a lion when they had attacked his flock. David affirmed, "The Lord that delivered me out of the paw of the lion, and out of the paw of the bear, he will deliver me out of the hand of this Philistine" (1 Sam. 17:37).[3] Saul was convinced and said to David, "Go, and the Lord be with thee."

With his shepherd's staff in hand, David went toward the giant. He stopped at a brook and selected five stones for his sling. The stones had been worn smooth and round by the torrents of spring that had rolled them down from the mountains. The giant, seeing David dressed as a shepherd but marching toward him, called out, "Am I a dog, that thou comest to me with staves?" (1 Sam. 17:43).

David replied, "This day will the Lord deliver thee into mine hand . . . that all the earth may know that there is a God in Israel" (1 Sam. 17:46).

"David put his hand in his bag, and took thence a stone, and slang it" (1 Sam. 17:49). Did he just sling it toward the Philistine, or did he aim at a specific spot? According to Judges 20:16, "There were seven hundred chosen men lefthanded; every one could sling stones at an hair breadth, and not miss." Rabbi Tanchum affirmed that they "could aim at a hair and hit it." Therefore, we can reasonably conclude that David purposely aimed at the giant's forehead, the one vital spot unprotected by his armor. "The stone sunk into his forehead; and he fell upon his face to the earth" (1 Sam. 17:49). David then used the giant's own sword to behead him (1 Sam. 17:51).

So great a victory was won so simply because God was pleased with David, who was willing to use the talent he had and trust Jehovah to do the rest. Likewise when we use what talent we have for the glory of our God and trust Him, He will give the victory over evil. He will supply freely what we cannot.[4]

To the victor go the spoils. Therefore, "David took the head of the Philistine, and brought it to Jerusalem" (1 Sam. 17:54). This verse is an excellent example of how the Bible cuts through years and states the final act as if it were done immediately. David actually took the head of Goliath to Jerusalem years later, after he had captured the Jebusite city and made it his capital. The giant's sword and armor were first placed with the tabernacle at Nob. It was from there that David later claimed the sword and made it his own.

Needless to say, Saul was impressed. He had taken little notice of David in the past and therefore couldn't even remember his family and tribal heritage. Now he was forced to ask, "Whose son art thou?" (1 Sam. 17:58).

Even though David was not of the tribe of Benjamin, Saul's tribe, Saul made him his armor-bearer and took him into his family because he "behaved himself wisely" (1 Sam. 18:5).[5] The royal servants and all the people also liked David. There was even a popular song that praised David above Saul. Two lines of the song's lyrics stated, "Saul hath slain his thousands,/and David his ten thousands" (1 Sam. 18:7).[6] David was the national hero! In a short time, without coverage by television or newspapers, David had gone from being just a shepherd lad to being the darling of Israel.[7]

Putting Truth into Action

1. What quality of David's helped keep him humble before God?
2. What motivation led David to do battle with Goliath?
3. What "giants" are you facing today—strained relationships, financial difficulties, or something else— and what lessons from David's victory over Goliath might help you in tackling them?
4. Expand on the statement "We should study David so that we might have a richer appreciation of Jesus."
5. Discuss why it is most difficult for one to secure support from one's own relatives and home town people.

SAUL'S ISRAEL SURROUNDED BY ENEMIES

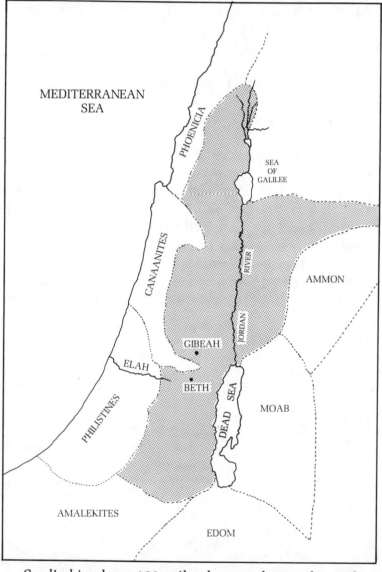

Saul's kingdom, 160 miles long and 50 miles wide, was both surrounded by and infiltrated by enemies.

CHAPTER 2

Victim of Jealousy

1 Samuel 18:8 through 21:15

Jealousy is a cancer that eats away at a person, destroying his ability to enjoy even the legitimate successes of others. A good example comes from the life of Sir John Gielgud, the superb Shakespearean actor. He once remarked, "I don't really know what jealousy is." But after thinking a bit longer, he said, "Oh, yes, I do! I remember! When Larry [Olivier] had a success as Hamlet, I wept." Despite his own great success on the stage, he couldn't bear the thought of another actor's excelling in a role he had played. Solomon truthfully said "Envy [is] the rottenness of the bones" (Prov. 14:30).

King Saul was also gripped by jealousy, an envy so deep that he was driven to homicidal rage. He became incensed when he heard the song praising David: "They have ascribed unto David ten thousands, and to me they have ascribed but thousands: and what can he have more but the kingdom?" (1 Sam. 18:8). From that time on, he looked with jealousy at David and eventually sought his life. How quickly the mind can change when its precious self-image is perceived to be threatened!

The dark brooding that had so often troubled Saul soon turned into open raving, because the evil spirit that had replaced the Holy Spirit was upon him.[1] One day as David was playing the harp to soothe Saul, the king thought, *I will nail David to the wall with my spear.* Saul hurled his spear, but David sprang aside. Saul then threw his javelin, and again David avoided it.

Then Saul grew afraid of David, because he knew Jehovah was with him (1 Sam. 18:12). He removed David from his court and placed him over a thousand soldiers. In his new position, David was often before the people of Israel, and he always behaved himself wisely. Thus he gained the respect and love of his men and of all the people of Israel.

This only compounded Saul's fear (1 Sam. 18:9), and he wanted David dead more than ever. But knowing the people loved David, he resorted to a cunning plan. "Let not mine hand be upon him," he said, "but let the hand of the Philistines be upon him" (1 Sam. 18:17). The plot? "Be thou valiant for me," Saul said to David as he promised him the hand of his elder daughter, Merab, in marriage if he accomplished certain exceedingly dangerous missions. And when David and his men successfully carried out the missions, David found that Saul had already given Merab to another man.

The king then offered David a second daughter, Michal, if he would bring him, in the place of the customary dowry, a hundred Philistine foreskins. David and his men slew and circumcised two hundred Philistines and brought the bloody foreskins to Saul (1 Sam. 18:25-27).[2] Then "Saul gave him Michal his daughter to wife. And Saul saw and knew that the Lord was with David, and that Michal Saul's daughter loved him" (1 Sam. 18:27-28).

Saul next tried to enlist the help of his son Jonathan to help slay David. Why, if he knew Jehovah was with David, did he keep trying to kill him? The combination of jealousy and fear simply made him irrational.

Upon hearing his father's request, Jonathan made an excellent defense of his friend David that brought peace to his father's tormented mind. But after a time the evil spirit prevailed, and Saul again "sought to smite David even to the wall with the javelin; but he slipped away . . . and escaped that night" (1 Sam. 19:10).

David went to his own house and into the arms of his loving wife. He was safe only for a moment, because Saul sent scouts with orders to guard against David's escape and to slay him in the morning. But Michal, knowing her father, warned her husband to flee and lowered David through a window into the darkness and out of her life. In this act of heart-wrenching devotion to her husband, Michal portrayed the truly heroic wife of every age. How different Michal was here in her relationship to David than years later when next we hear her speak to David! Time and circumstances often warp the most beautiful of relationships into grotesque mockeries.

David was now a homeless outlaw from the court of King Saul, and thus he would remain for the next seven long, lean years.

Writing about the night of his escape in Psalm 59, David said,

> Deliver me from mine enemies, O my God: defend
> me from them that rise up against me. . . . The mighty
> are gathered against me; not for my transgression,
> nor for my sin, O Lord. They run and prepare

themselves without my fault. . . . Consume them . . .
and let them know that God ruleth in Jacob unto the
ends of the earth. . . . But I will sing of thy power;
yea, I will sing aloud of thy mercy in the morning:
for thou has been my defense and refuge in the day
of my trouble. (vv. 1, 3, 13, 16)

David was going to feel the need for prayer many
times during the following years as he fled from
place to place to escape the envy of Saul. His faith
would be tested repeatedly. Would he continue to
praise Jehovah's loving-kindness as he did in Psalm
59?

DAVID FLEES TO SAMUEL

David fled from Gibeah, Saul's hometown and
provisional capital, to Ramah, which was about six
miles north in the mountains. He dwelt with Samuel
for a period of time during which, it seems certain,
he was taught much by this old and wise judge.

Saul was informed where David was and sent
"messengers," likely armed soldiers, to capture him,
but God built a spiritual hedge around Ramah.
When Saul or anyone sent from him approached
Ramah, he would become so filled with the Holy
Spirit that he would begin to proclaim God's holy
word and thus be rendered harmless to David.

It is thought that David composed Psalm 11 at
Ramah. It reads: "In the Lord I put my trust: how
say ye to my soul, Flee as a bird to your mountain?
For, lo, the wicked bend their bow, they make ready
their arrow upon the string, that they may privily
shoot at the upright in heart. If the foundations be
destroyed, what can the righteous do?" (vv. 1-3).

The expression "if the foundations be destroyed" asks an important question: When the established government, society, or age crumbles all around you, where can you flee? The answer is, to the mountain of God, for it is a solid refuge forever. Not only in this psalm but throughout the Bible, righteous people are taught that even though we place our trust in God, He expects us to escape from danger if we can and not to make deliberate martyrs of ourselves.

In addition, verse 6 of the psalm contains the first use in the Bible of the word *cup* as a metaphor for one's lot in life: "Fire and brimstone, and a horrible tempest: this shall be the portion of their cup." Christ used this figure of speech when He prayed, "O my Father, if it be possible, let this cup [His crucifixion] pass from me: nevertheless not as I will, but as thou wilt" (Matt. 26:39). Read also how Christ used this metaphor in Matthew 20:22-23 and John 18:11.

DAVID AND JONATHAN

David, seeing that Saul would not give him peace at Ramah, went south to Gibeah, where he had a conference with his friend Jonathan. "What have I done? . . . that he seeketh my life?" he asked (1 Sam. 20:1). Jonathan didn't know the extent of his father's evil envy and so was not aware of David's imminent danger. But David assured him "there is but a step between me and death" (1 Sam. 20:3). The two friends then devised a plan by which Jonathan could determine his father's true intent toward David and agreed to rendezvous in three days.

On the second day after the friends had met, Saul asked about David. When Jonathan spoke defensively of David, his father hurled a spear at him. Saul told him that as long as David lived, he (Jonathan) would not be established as the king of Israel. Jonathan already knew this, yet he did not envy David (1 Sam. 20:13-15).

Jonathan's claim to our affection rests in his selfless friendship to David. He was as John the Baptizer was toward Jesus in the New Testament in that their motto could have been, "you, the unknown, must increase, and I, the established, must decrease" (paraphrase of John 3:30).

Jonathan, shaken and angry, left his father, and at the appointed time he met David. They wept together and comforted one another. Jonathan said to David, "Go in peace, forasmuch as we have sworn both of us in the name of the Lord, saying, The Lord be between me and thee, and between my seed and thy seed for ever" (1 Sam. 20:42). Many years later, David did remember this pledge and blessed the seed of Jonathan. Dean Stanley wrote of Jonathan and David, "Each found in the other the affection that he found not in his own family."

DAVID VISITS THE HIGH PRIEST

David then turned away from his wife, his friend, his exalted position, and Samuel. If he ever saw Samuel again, it is not recorded. How heavy must have been his heart! Alone and no place to go. He dared not return to his boyhood home in Bethlehem, because Jonathan had led Saul to believe he was there to give him time to escape. David was now a hunted outlaw with the decree of death on his head. He went to Nob, where the tabernacle of Jehovah was and where the priests lived. He inquired of God for guidance through the high priest Ahimelech. This inquiring of God would begin a righteous pattern of going to God for advice and support before every important undertaking. Jesus, the son of David, also followed this practice, and if the Savior prayed before making a decision, how much more do we need to inquire of God?

Seeing David without a military detachment, Ahimelech was surprised and frightened. To Ahimelech's question, "Why art thou alone?" David replied that Saul had told him, "Let no man know anything of the business whereabout I send thee" (1 Sam. 21:2). David's answer was a self-protecting statement that had no basis in truth.[3]

After reaching Nob and being joined by a group of young men, David expressed the need for food and weapons. He asked Ahimelech to supply both, explaining that because of haste he had brought neither. It is possible that he had not eaten during those three anxious days of waiting for word from Jonathan. As for the "young men" stated to be with him, we know nothing.

At Nob, which is only four miles south of Gibeah, Ahimelech, the eighty-five priests with him, and their families had only the hallowed shewbread from the tabernacle to eat. This seems a clear commentary on the poor state of Jehovah's priests in Saul's day and the low esteem given to the law of Moses. If, as the Bible scholar William Deane points out, tithes had been duly paid and offerings made, such destitution could not have occurred.

This shewbread was old, having been before Jehovah for a week before being replaced by fresh bread (1 Sam. 21:6). Even so, this stale bread was not for David and the young men with him to eat, because they were not priests (Lev. 24:5-9). However, David didn't believe in living by the "letter of the law" that kills (2 Cor. 3:6), but through the Spirit of God, who loves and cares for humanity. He asked the priest for five loaves of the week-old bread, and Ahimelech complied. Jesus justified David's actions centuries later and used the incident to show that it was correct for His disciples to pick ears of corn as they passed through the fields on the Sabbath (Mark 2:23-28; see also Matt. 12:1-8).

The only weapon available to meet David's other need was the sword of Goliath, which David had undoubtedly placed in the tabernacle as an offering to God after God had given him the victory over the giant. The high priest offered it to David, and he was pleased to have it back, saying, "There is none like that." As David was talking to the high priest, he probably noticed a servant of Saul, Doeg, watching him, and he knew that the eyes of Saul were everywhere in Israel. Thus, "David arose, and fled that day for fear of Saul, and went to Achish the king of Gath" (1 Sam. 21:10).

DAVID DECEIVES THE KING OF GATH

Gath was one of the five principal cities of the Philistines. Its exact location has been lost for millennia, but it is supposed to have been located some thirty miles southwest of Nob. David probably covered twice that distance following the circuitous roads of his day and avoided cities where Saul might be looking for him. Gath was populated by the Gittites and had been the home of Goliath. David apparently thought that for some reason he would not be recognized as Goliath's killer, and he planned to offer his services to King Achish.

David was recognized by the servants of Achish, however, who thought David had already become the king of Israel. David, overhearing these remarks, was frightened and reacted in a most inventive way, showing his genius and versatility. "He changed his behavior before them, and feigned himself mad in their hands, and scrabbled on the doors of the gate, and let his spittle fall down upon his beard" (1 Sam. 21:13). Achish, deceived by David's act, responded by sending David away, declaring he had no lack of mad men around him already.

This narrow escape prompted David to compose two psalms that show the true, inner David: frightened, alone, but with full trust in Jehovah's power to save. Psalm 56 begins with David's appealing for God's mercy because he felt his enemies were trying to swallow him. Twice he said, in verses 3-4 and 10-11 he was not afraid of what man could do unto him as he had put his trust in God.

Can we say as David said, "This I know; for God is for me" (v. 9)? Read Romans 8:28-39 for the joy that divine assurance can bring. "If God has begun a good work in us, he will carry it through to the end," said W. Forsyth, an Old Testament scholar, and David knew God had anointed him for a purpose. He took hold of God's strength and was strong. Can we not do the same?[4]

Psalm 34, written about the same incident, begins, "I will bless the Lord at all times." The righteous must praise God on the cloudy day as well as the sunny. The psalm continues, "The angel of the Lord encampeth round about them that fear him, and delivereth them" (v. 7). The following examples demonstrate God's angelic protection of His people: Genesis 31:22-32:2, where God warned Laban not to harm his son-in-law Jacob, who had left Padan-aram to return to Canaan. Only after their encounter was safely over were Jacob's eyes opened so that he saw the host of angels there to protect him. And read 2 Kings 6:8-23, where Elisha was surrounded by an invisible army of horses and chariots of fire.

If we follow God, we are never alone and can affirm along with David, "O taste and see that the Lord is good" (Psa. 34:8).

David turned to instruction in verses 12-14, asking "What man is he that desireth life, and loveth many days, that he may see good?" His response was, "Keep thy tongue from evil, and thy lips from speaking guile. Depart from evil, and do good; seek peace, and pursue it." Peace is not simply the absence of strife but the presence of goodness which must be pursued actively.[5]

Putting Truth into Action

1. How have you seen jealousy affect others? Yourself?

2. How do we inquire of God for guidance in making decisions today?

3. We've seen David lie several times to protect himself. When, if ever, might lying be acceptable for us, and what guidelines should we follow?

4. When may the principle be applied today that justified David's eating of the shewbread?

CHAPTER 3

Suffering for God

1 Samuel 22:1 through 26:25

Why does a loving God allow good people to suffer? This question has troubled human minds for thousands of years. Entire books have been written to try to answer it, and still we labor to understand. But one good answer can be found in David's experience as he continued to run from Saul's murderous hatred.

David could find no peace in or out of Israel. After escaping from Gath, he went into an almost uninhabited area where limestone hills formed a labyrinth of narrow valleys, the sides of which were honeycombed with caves. Rejected and dejected, David dwelt in one of the caves, the cave of Adullam, and wrote Psalm 142. There he reached the deepest depths of loneliness, crying, "I cried unto the Lord. . . . my spirit was overwhelmed within me. . . . refuge failed me; *no man cared for my soul*. . . . I am brought very low" (Psa. 142:1-6, emphasis added).

Being alone is not loneliness. Loneliness is when one feels no warming love, knows no sheltering friendship, sees no caring smile. That kind of loneliness can be traumatic, because we were not created to be isolated, islands in a cold, dark ocean.

However, even in the blackness of a wild cave, David knew there was one who cared, for he wrote, "I cried unto thee, O Lord: I said, Thou art my refuge and my portion in the land of the living" (v. 5). He asked God to deliver him from his persecutors and to bring his soul out of prison so that he might give thanks to His name. After praying, David felt so assured that in the last verse of the psalm, he declared he would have to be lonely no more, because God would deal bountifully with him. And hereafter, he would be surrounded by righteous friends.

Does prayer in time of need give us assurance? If not, it's because we don't know (by faith), as David did, that God is for us and loves us. We are never alone. Not only does God love us, but Christ also cares, the Holy Spirit pleads for us, and the angelic host of heaven and Christians on earth are concerned for us. Loneliness is not our portion unless we choose to turn our backs on the spiritual hosts surrounding us.

THE TURNING POINT

David's assurance was well-founded. Not only were his enemies seeking him, but so were his family and friends. God saw to it that David's friends heard where he was, and "they went down thither to him" (1 Sam. 22:1). Soon he was the leader of about 400 men (1 Sam. 22:2), and later of 600 (1 Sam. 23:13).

On other down days at the cave in Adullam, David wrote two more psalms. Psalm 57 is a prayer for mercy that ends in triumphant praise to God. It is easily divided into two parts by the refrain found in verses 5 and 11: "Be thou exalted, O God, above the heavens; let thy glory be above all the earth." This psalm is considered a twin to Psalm 56.

It was a reflection of the true David when he stated, "In the shadow of thy wings will I make my refuge, until these calamities be overpast" (v. 1). Often, in the following pages about David's life, we will marvel at his patient endurance. He was willing to wait, knowing God "performeth all things for me" in the fullness of time.

DAVID SUFFERS WITH CHRIST

In the title of Psalm 22 (the other psalm written in the cave), the Hebrew phrase "Aijeleth hash-Shahar" is found. It means "in the hind [early] hours of the morning." How often it is darkest just before the dawn! A mystery is the most perplexing before the first revealing ray of light that leads to the full disclosure of truth. David knew God had anointed him for a holy mission, yet now, "a reproach among men," he cried out, "My God, my God, why hast thou forsaken me?" (v. 1). These are the very words our Savior uttered on the cross in the darkest hour of His life (Matt. 27:46). Thus begins one of the grandest outbursts of prophetic inspiration in the Bible. David became the voice of his far-in-the-future son, the Savior. "All they that see me laugh me to scorn: they shoot out the lip, they shake the head, saying, He trusted on the Lord that he would deliver him: let him deliver him, seeing he delighted in him" (vv. 7-8). Just as David was when he pretended insanity, Christ was mocked and ridiculed before

His crucifixion and while hanging on the cross. "They that passed by railed on him, wagging their heads, and saying, Ah, thou that destroyest the temple, and buildest it in three days, Save thyself, and come down from the cross" (Mark 15:29-30; see also Matt. 27:39-44; Mark 15:16-20; Luke 23:35-39).

David, feeling fully the agony his Savior must bear for him, sobbed, "I am poured out like water, and all my bones are out of joint" (v. 14). Both water and blood poured from our Savior's side, and the stress of hanging on the cross caused His joints to become dislocated. David continued, "My heart is like wax; it is melted in the midst of my bowels" (v. 14). Often the strain of crucifixion on the heart caused it literally to rupture. Did Christ die of a broken heart because of you and me? "My strength is dried up like a potsherd; and my tongue cleaveth to my jaws" (v. 15). "I thirst," cried Jesus, because He knew "that all things were now accomplished, that the prophecy might be fulfilled" (John 19:28).

In verse 16, David cried, "They pierced my hands and my feet." What a picture the Holy Spirit showed David of the Savior's sufferings! If God allowed His Son to suffer that we might be ransomed, then God indeed loves us and will not let us go. If we are disciples of Christ, we are anointed ones as was David; we have been chosen for a mission as was David; and we are destined for success as was David. But we must have David's submissive faith, for God will not make us succeed against our will.

The psalm continues, "They part my garments among them, and cast lots upon my vesture" (v. 18). This specific prophecy, fulfilled over 900 years later at the death of Jesus (as recorded in John 19:23-24 and Matt. 27:35), is proof of the inspiration of David, the divinity of Jesus, and the almighty foreknowledge of God the Father.

After the feelings of rejection expressed through most of verse 21, David suddenly exclaimed, "Thou hast heard me." Knowing he had been heard by God, David shifted from a prayer for God's mercy to a praise for God's deliverance—from gloom to victory in a phrase. In verse 22 he exclaimed, "I will declare thy name unto my brethren: in the midst of the congregation will I praise thee."[1] This verse is quoted as the words of Christ in Hebrews 2:12, part of that splendid chapter that explains why our Savior suffered such agony for us.

In the second part of Psalm 22, verses 22-31, David described the glorious kingdom of Jesus. It will be universal: "all the Kindreds of the nations shall worship before thee. For the kingdom is the Lord's: and he is the governor among the nations" (vv. 27-28). It will be spread, not by might of arms, but by the gospel of Christ: "They shall come, and shall declare his righteousness unto a people that shall be born, that he hath done this" (v. 31). In other words, the Gentiles will be told that Christ died for their sins, and they will be born spiritually by baptism into God's family.

In a much lighter vein let us note that in verse 21 the old King James version mistranslated a non-existent animal into existence. "From the horns of the unicorns," but the New King James has laid it to rest by properly translating it "wild oxen."

DAVID DEVELOPS HIS STAFF

Meanwhile, back at the cave, David was molding

his growing band of men; men distressed by Saul's cruel injustices, and those discontented and bitter of soul. They came from every tribe of Israel, plus Moabites, Hittites and Gibeonites. David molded them into an ancient Robin Hood's band of which some became the "mighty men" whose names and astounding deeds are recorded in 2 Samuel 23:8-39 and 1 Chronicles 11:10-47.[2]

David, like Christ, had a magnetic personality attracting followers from a wide spectrum of professions. To fulfill his destiny, David would need a prophet to proclaim God's will, a priest to offer sacrifices to the Lord and to give His blessings, and a chronicler to record the historical moments of the period. Men to fill these needs were drawn to him.

The prophet was Gad, who said to David, "Abide not in the hold; depart, and get thee into the land of Judah" (1 Sam. 22:5). Gad may well have been an acquaintance of David's sent from the school of prophets in Ramah by Samuel. He became the seer to David and his biographer (1 Chron. 29:29; 2 Chron. 29:25).

The priest was Abiathar, the son of Ahimelech, who came to join David because of the cruelty of Saul. After Doeg had told Saul of seeing David with the high priest at Nob, Saul questioned Ahimelech and accused him and all the priests of being on David's side. In his insane anger, he ordered his servants to kill them all. When the servants would not slay the priests, Saul turned to Doeg, who killed not only Ahimelech, but eighty-four other priests as well. Furthermore, in his bloodthirstiness he went to Nob and killed the wives, children, and animals of the priests. Only Abiathar escaped, and he then became the chief priest in David's court. "And David said unto Abiathar, I knew it that day, when Doeg the Edomite was there, that he would surely tell Saul: I have occasioned the death of all the persons of thy father's house. Abide thou with me, fear not: for he that seeketh my life seeketh thy life: but with me thou shalt be in safe guard" (1 Sam. 22:22-23).

Psalm 52 is addressed to Doeg as a bearer of false witness. David wrote that God would destroy him and that the righteous would learn from his destruction. In the last two verses, David contrasted himself with Doeg: "I am like a green olive tree in the house of God." He wrote that he would trust in God, give thanks to God, and put his hope in Him.

David knew his life would be hectic as long as Saul sought to kill him. Therefore, he requested of the king of Moab, "Let my father and my mother . . . be with you, till I know what God will do for me" (1 Sam. 22:3). It was logical that David chose Moab as a sanctuary for his parents, because both he and his father had Moabite blood in their veins from their foremother Ruth.

David provided for his parents even as Christ on the cross provided for His mother (John 19:26-27). The Bible strongly teaches children to provide for their parents, whether they are the oldest son, as Christ was, or the youngest, as David was. Jesus condemned the Pharisees for trying to weasel out of their duty to their parents (Matt. 15:3-9). We cannot expect the government or anyone else to relieve us of our duty to our fathers and mothers.

While entrusting his parents to the king of Moab, David entrusted himself to God with the words, "Till I know what God will do for me." What a wonderful statement of faith for a young man of perhaps twenty-two! It's wonderful for a man or woman of any age to be able to say, "I will wait for Jehovah. I will not try to rush Him or become discouraged if He takes longer than I think correct." David said in Psalm 31:15, "My times are in thy hand."

DAVID LEARNS A HARD LESSON

To furnish food and supplies for his followers, David had to provide protection where the government of Saul did not, and he knew that in the unprotected lowland of Judah stood the city of Keilah. It was harvest time, and roving bands of Philistines were "robbing the threshing floors." If David and his army fought off the Philistines, he could expect the grateful citizens of Keilah to repay his protective army with grain. But before he moved toward rescuing Keilah, he "inquired of the Lord saying, Shall I go and smite these Philistines? And the Lord said unto David, Go, and smite the Philistines, and save Keilah" (1 Sam. 23:2). David was ready to move, but his men were afraid, reasoning that with King Saul and the army of Israel already against them, incurring the wrath of the Philistines would make life doubly hard. David then inquired of Jehovah a second time, and this time Jehovah probably replied openly for the benefit of the men, "I will deliver the Philistines into thine hand" (1 Sam. 23:4). So David and his men saved Keilah from famine and likely a worse fate of pillage, rape, and enslavement by defeating the Philistines.

Saul heard of David's victory and felt God had delivered David into his hands. If he could only surround Keilah, he could trap David inside the

fortifications. However, David also had spies, who
reported Saul's plans to him. After hearing of Saul's
intentions, David bade Abiathar to bring the ephod
that he might ask God if Saul would really destroy
a whole city just to capture him.[3] God answered in
the affirmative. David asked another question that
reflected his ever-growing understanding of human
nature: "Will the men of Keilah deliver me and my
men into the hand of Saul?" God said, "They will
deliver thee up" (1 Sam. 23:12). It's a sad commentary on mankind that often self-good is placed before
a moral obligation, and self-preservation overrides
gratefulness.

David was forced to flee to the wilderness of Ziph.
But even there, the inhabitants, who were brethren
of David and part of the tribe of Judah, reported to
Saul that David was among them. Saul was delighted
and told the Ziphites to watch David closely because
he had heard that "he dealeth very subtilly" (1 Sam.
23:22). Then Saul and his army, leaving Gibeah
unprotected, marched south to Ziph. In spite of
David's efforts to escape, Saul's army encompassed
him and his men. Just as Saul was about to close
in for the kill, there came an urgent message for
Saul from Gibeah: "Haste thee, and come; for the
Philistines have invaded the land" (1 Sam. 23:27).
Saul withdrew, and the Lord delivered David once
again.

Psalm 54 was written after the above occasion. It
begins with a cry for help and ends with a thanks
for deliverance.

DAVID SPARES SAUL

David then moved his army to the rugged western boundary of the Dead Sea, an area known as En-gedi. But he wasn't safe even there, because after Saul had defeated the Philistines in the north, he took a select force of 3,000 men and again headed south to find David.

David and some of his men sought shelter in the recesses of a cave. Later, Saul entered the cave alone to relieve himself, or, as the polite Hebrew expression put it, "to cover his feet" (1 Sam. 24:3). Coming from the outside light into the darkness of the cave, Saul could not see David, but David and his men, their eyes accustomed to the darkness, could easily see Saul. Saul was in no position to defend himself; therefore, it seemed certain to David's men that he had been delivered into David's hands by the Lord. David quietly came near Saul and cut off the skirt of the outer garment Saul had tossed aside, but then his conscience smote him. He retreated into the recesses of the cave and explained to his men, "The Lord forbid that I should . . . stretch forth mine hand against him, seeing he is the anointed of the Lord" (1 Sam. 24:6). David had to restrain some of his men, however, who did not have consciences as finely tuned to God's will as his own.

The good person always fights with a handicap in that he cannot take advantage of unethical tactics or wicked opportunities. As Shakespeare well wrote:

> O Opportunity! thy guilt is great;
> 'Tis thou that execut'st the traitor's reason;
> Thou set'st the wolf where he the lamb may get;
> Whoever plots the sin, thou point'st the season;

> 'Tis thou that spurn'st at right, at law, at reason;
> And in thy shady cell, where none may spy him,
> Sits sin, to seize the souls that wander by him.

The righteous hero may fight at a disadvantage, but with God on his side, who can successfully be against him? (Romans 8:31).

The Lord had given David both an opportunity and a test, for the one seeking his life was helpless before him. But David knew it was not his right to harm one anointed by God. The judgment of Saul was wholly in God's hands. When we consider that Christians today are God's anointed, how careful we should be not to condemn, not to harm!

David followed Saul from the cave, still carrying the skirt of Saul's cloak in his hand. How startled the king must have been when from behind him he heard the words, "My lord the king. . . . Behold, this day thine eyes have seen how that the Lord had delivered thee today into mine hand in the cave: and some bade me kill thee: but mine eye spared thee; and I said, I will not put forth mine hand against my lord; for he is the Lord's anointed. . . . See the skirt of thy robe in my hand: for . . . I cut off the skirt of thy robe, and killed thee not" (1 Sam. 24:8-11). David, in this rather long address, appealed to the truth of a proverb already ancient in his day: "Wickedness proceedeth from the wicked" (1 Sam. 24:13).

David closed his remarks to Saul by saying, "The Lord therefore be judge, and judge between me and thee, . . . and deliver me out of thine hand" (1 Sam. 24:15).

A convicted Saul wept before David and cried out, "Thou art more righteous than I: for thou hast rewarded me good, whereas I have rewarded thee evil. . . . I know well that thou shalt surely be king, and that the kingdom of Israel shall be established in thine hand" (1 Sam. 24:17, 20). However, having acknowledged the truth, Saul did nothing to hasten the day when David would become king. He and his army went away, leaving David and his men in the wilderness to await the next round.

Two psalms are assigned to this time in En-gedi, Psalm 7 and Psalm 35. Psalm 35 is closely aligned with David's speech to Saul.[4] He pleaded his "righteous cause" (v. 27) and prayed to God to deliver him from those who "rewarded me evil for good" (v. 12).

In Psalm 7, David's theme was "God as the righteous judge is my refuge." He pleaded with God to judge his righteousness and the "integrity that is in me" (v. 8). He wrote, "Yea, I have delivered him that without cause is mine enemy" (v. 4), referring to his allowing Saul to go free. There is one phrase in this psalm we should all remember: "The righteous God trieth the hearts and reins" (v. 9).

A LESSON IN PATIENCE

While David was still at En-gedi, Samuel died. David was around twenty-six years of age, and Saul had two years to live before God's vengeance would end his wasted life.

After Saul returned to Gibeah, David and his men moved westward into Paran, the area from which Moses sent the twelve spies northward into the promised land (Num. 13). There David's army returned to protecting Israelite villages and herdsmen from marauding bands of heathens. Since David was of the tribe of Judah, he was among his own, but kinship had not always proved a protection. By now he was also well known far and near, among Israelites and heathens, for his mighty deeds. His ruptured relationship with Saul was common knowledge, and the fact that he would be the next king of Israel was acknowledged by many of the elders. So he and his men were generally well-received.

At this point in David's life comes a story of his dealings with a rich but worthless man by the name of Nabal. This story is seemingly unrelated to the main story of David's wait for the crown but it shows us how Jehovah was training David, teaching him the lessons he would need to learn before he became king of God's chosen people. In this incident, David was taught not to avenge himself but to control his temper, avoid blood-guiltiness, and allow God's will to follow its determined course.

As mentioned, David and his men were generally well-received by the people, who gave gifts of food for their protection. But when David sent ten of his men to Nabal to wish him well and ask for a gift of food, they were rebuffed with this statement: "Who is David? . . . there be many servants nowadays that break away every man from his master. Shall I then take my bread, and my water, and my flesh that I have killed for my shearers, and give it unto men, whom I know not whence they be?" (1 Sam. 25:10-11). Shocked, the ten young men reported to David. He was infuriated at the insult to himself and to the Lord God. "Gird ye on every man his sword" shouted David. "Surely in vain have I kept all that this fellow hath . . . he hath requited me evil for good. So and more also do God unto the enemies of David, if I leave . . . to him by the morning light any that pisseth against the wall" (1 Sam. 25:13, 21-22).

Who was this Nabal against whom David swore such a fearful vow? He was a descendant of Caleb who possessed 3,000 sheep and 1,000 goats. He was, according to the meaning of his name, and according to his wife and his servants, a headstrong fool who was evil in his doings. Unlike Nabal, his wife Abigail was both beautiful and intelligent.

After David's men left Nabal, a servant went to Abigail and rehearsed the exchange between David's messengers and Nabal. She immediately collected a gracious gift of food to give to David and sent it ahead of her, for she determined to go to David and beg for mercy. When Abigail saw David, she quickly dismounted, bowed low to the ground at his feet, and began to reason with him. She freely admitted to the churlish behavior of her husband but pleaded with David, saying,

> The Lord will certainly make my lord a sure house; because my lord fighteth the battles of the Lord, and evil hath not been found in thee all thy days. Yet a man is risen to pursue thee, and to seek thy soul: but the soul of my lord shall be bound in the bundle of life with the Lord thy God; and the souls of thine enemies, them shall he sling out, as out of the middle of a sling. And it shall come to pass, when the Lord shall have done to my lord according to all the good that he hath spoken concerning thee, and shall have appointed thee ruler over Israel; that this shall be no grief unto thee, nor offence of heart unto my lord, either that thou hast shed blood causeless, or that my lord hath avenged himself: but when the Lord shall have dealt well with my lord, then remember thine handmaid.[5]

David accepted her gift and her advice and sent her to her house in peace, saying, "Blessed be the Lord God of Israel, which sent thee this day to meet me: and blessed be thy advice, and blessed be thou, which hast kept me this day from coming to shed blood, and from avenging myself with mine own hand" (1 Sam. 25:32-33).

After placating David, Abigail returned to her husband and found him drunk from a feast he had held to celebrate his prosperous season. The morning after the feast, when the merriness of the wine wore off, she told him what she had done. He had a heart attack, leaving him paralyzed "as a stone" for ten days before the Lord flung him "as from a sling."

Like the prosperous but selfish farmer in Jesus' parable in Luke 12:16-21, Nabal was wealthy but "not rich toward God."

God had taught David not only to control his temper, avoid blood-guiltiness, and to "wait upon Jehovah," but also the sanctity of being for the right. That righteousness is above one's duty to parents we have already learned from Michal and Jonathan. From Abigail's actions, we learn that being for the right—on God's side—is above loyalty to one's spouse. David's decision not to carry out his vow to destroy Nabal's family teaches there is a higher law than that imposed by a vow. If one makes a foolish or hasty vow that is wrong and then learns what is right, he is released from keeping the unrighteous promise and thus compounding his sin. Being right with God must take precedence over all other duties and obligations.

Hunted Again

With time, Saul's gratitude to David for not taking his life in the cave had worn off. He gave Michal, David's first wife and Saul's daughter, to another man, and he was ready once again to seek David's life. When the people of Ziph reported a second time the whereabouts of David, Saul took 3,000 men and marched south.

David's spies kept him informed of Saul's location. With this information, he moved his men in close, and by night he and Abishai went into the very heart of the army of Israel. The wagons filled with provisions had been formed into a barricade, and in the midst lay Saul, sleeping. Abner, Saul's general, was close by to protect the king.

Abishai requested permission to kill Saul, but David refused him, saying, "Who can stretch forth his hand against the Lord's anointed, and be guiltless?" (1 Sam. 26:9). David had steeled himself to wait for Saul to die in one of three ways: God would smite him, he would die naturally, or he would be killed in battle. It was to be the third way.

David took Saul's spear, which was stuck in the ground at his head, and his jar of water. He and Abishai then left, thinking how quiet and crafty they had been. In actuality, God had protected them by causing a deep sleep to fall upon Saul and his entire army.

From the top of a mountain far off, David shouted to Saul and Abner, calling attention to the missing spear and water jar. He rebuked Abner for not giving better protection to Saul (1 Sam. 26:15-16).

In reply, Saul admitted he had sinned toward David and asked David to return with him to Gibeah, saying he would do no more harm.[6] David did not respond to the invitation but called on God to deliver him out of all tribulation. Saul closed this last face-to-face meeting between himself and David with these prophetic words: "Blessed be thou, my son David: thou shalt both do great things, and also shalt still prevail" (1 Sam. 26:25).

Putting Truth into Action

1. What lessons did David learn through his suffering? What lessons might God be trying to teach you through yours?

2. David refused to attack King Saul, God's anointed, even though Saul sought his life. What does this suggest about how we should treat other Christians, even those who make themselves our enemies?

3. When was a time you made a vow you later came to regret? What did you do? How might you handle the situation differently next time?

4. In today's society what obligations do grown children have toward their aging parents?

CHAPTER 4

Exaltation and Ruination

1 Samuel 27:1 through 2 Samuel 1
1 Chronicles 10

There's no such thing as standing still spiritually. We're either moving upward, closer to God, or downward, away from Him. Sometimes, of course, our progress looks like the title of the Charles Swindoll book: three steps forward, two steps back. But there's a basic direction in which we're moving at each point in time, even when we get off the track temporarily.

In the next stage of David's life, we see him and Saul moving in opposite directions. David was heading ever upward, while Saul was on the road to destruction. We can learn valuable lessons from both experiences.

David at Ziklag

In 1 Samuel 27 after escaping from Saul once more, David reasoned that if he remained on land controlled by Saul, he would one day die at his hand. Therefore, he "should speedily escape into the land of the Philistines," where Saul would despair of seeking him. This he, his men, and their families did. He arranged with King Achish of Gath to provide him with bounty from raids. In return, the Philistine lord gave David the city of Ziklag.

For the following year and four months, David made Ziklag the base of his operations. Plundering raids were made against the native inhabitants of the south, but David told Achish the raids were against Israelites. To insure his deception, "David saved neither man nor woman alive, to bring tidings to Gath, saying, Lest they should tell on us" (1 Sam. 27:11).

During this period, the ranks of David's followers grew until they were "like the host of God" (1 Chron. 12:22). Men came to him from the various tribes of Israel and from foreign tribes. Among the foreigners were Ittai the Gittite and Uriah the Hittite, who proved themselves in battle and became members of David's "mighty men," the first in battle and in loyalty to David throughout their lives.

This is a time in David's life to which no psalms are attributed. He seems to have been at his apogee with the Lord (1 Sam. 26:19).[1]

The Philistine tribes could clearly see the increasing signs of disorganization and weakness in Saul's Israel, so they decided to mount a major offensive. Their strategy was to march northward following the coastal plain, gathering additional troops as they marched, then turn inland through the valley of Megiddo and sweep southward through the heart of Israel. This Megiddo valley, also called Armageddon, was the same one where so many decisive battles were fought that by New Testament times it became a synonym for any great battle of decision (Rev. 16:16).

King Achish let David know he would be expected to march with the Philistine horde against Israel. David enigmatically answered, "Surely thou shalt know what thy servant can do" (1 Sam. 28:2). What would David do? He was buying time by agreeing to go, but when the battle was engaged, would he fight for the enemy of Israel or turn traitor to his benefactor? Clearly David was a good man in bad company, even as Peter was when he warmed himself at the Devil's fire during the trial of Jesus. It is truly comforting to see, in both cases, how tenderly God saves but disciplines His chosen when they wander from His side.

As the lords of the Philistines and their armies gathered, they saw a strange sight, an army of Hebrews in their midst. "Then said the princes of the Philistines, What do these Hebrews here? And Achish said unto the princes . . . , Is not this David, the servant of Saul the king of Israel, which hath been with me these days, or these years, and I have found no fault in him since he fell unto me unto this day?" (1 Sam. 29:3). The princes of the Philistines would not accept David, however, and demanded that Achish send him back to Ziklag, saying, "Lest in the battle he be an adversary to us." (1 Sam. 29:4). They well remembered that David was the celebrated hero of whom the Israelites sang, "Saul hath slain his thousands, and David his ten thousands,"

Achish apologized to David but told him he must turn back. David protested, but Achish was firm. So David and his men rose up early the next morning and marched back to Ziklag. God had rescued David yet again, but did David see the hand of God working on his behalf? No visible miracle was performed, yet the providential will of God was accomplished. We may not see His hand today, either, but we may rest assured that God has not abdicated control of His universe.

DAVID PURSUES THE AMALEKITES

When David and his army arrived back in Ziklag, they found only charred remains. The Amalekites had raided the city and taken all the wives and children captive. The predators had become the prey. No one could know better what horrors awaited their wives and children than these men of David who lived by plundering other villages. These men of blood now wept "until they had no more power to weep" (1 Sam. 30:4).

David was greatly distressed because his two wives had been taken captive, undoubtedly, to be sold into slavery. Beyond his personal grief, there was the grief of his followers, grief that turned to accusation and threats of stoning him. Deep grief so quickly becomes deep guilt, and guilt must have its sacrificial victim, even if it be self, a leader, or God. In times of tragedy, people often accuse God and curse Him rather than drawing close to Him for strength to bear their grief. David's men turned their hatred upon him. Maybe they felt it was David's fault because he had left Ziklag unprotected. Whatever the rationale, the guilt had been placed on him. A leader must know he will be assigned credit and glory or guilt and blame, and that the two may be separated only by a moment or an action.

David's schooling for leadership was hard. "For whom the Lord loveth he chasteneth, and scourgeth every son whom he receiveth" (Heb. 12:6; see also Prov. 3:12). The rod of the Lord was hard on David,

SOME CITIES AND GEOGRAPHIC AREAS MENTIONED IN THE BOOK

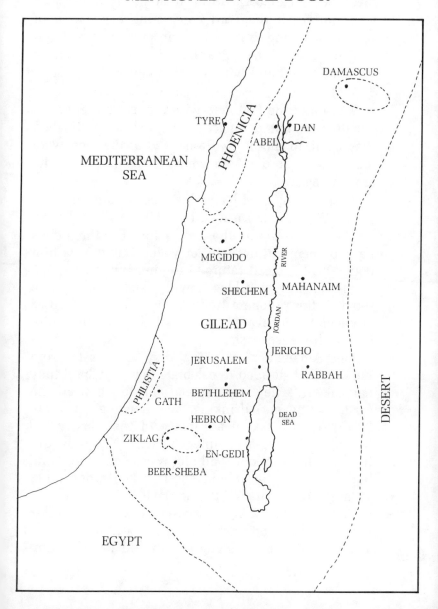

but it was needed because it turned him back to God. "David encouraged himself in the Lord his God" (1 Sam. 30:6). "I pray thee, bring me hither the ephod," called David to Abiathar the priest, and he inquired of the Lord concerning his course of action. Rejoicing to have His chosen son back, Jehovah answered him, "Pursue: for thou shalt surely overtake them, and without fail recover all" (1 Sam. 30:7-8).

David and the 600 men with him set out after the Amalekites, but the pace was grueling, and when they came to the brook Besor, 200 of the men were too weak to ford it and were left behind with the army's baggage.

Pressing on, David and his troops came upon a young Egyptian slave who had fallen sick and been left behind to die by the Amalekites. For three days he had been without food or water. David gave him both, and his spirit returned to him. When he spoke of the burning of Ziklag, David asked him to guide them to the pillaging troops. He agreed to serve as guide if David agreed not to kill him or turn him over to his past masters.

The Amalekites, thinking they were safe from pursuit, had stopped to celebrate the great spoil they had taken. "They were spread abroad upon all the earth, eating and drinking, and dancing" (1 Sam. 30:16). David, taking advantage of their laxity, attacked and won a complete victory. Not only did he and his men recover all that was taken from them, but also the flocks and herds taken from other villages. This extra spoil was David's.

David's jubilant men arrived back at the brook Besor and rejoined the 200 who had been left behind. The returning men, being selfish and lacking compassion, said of those who had remained with the baggage, "Because they went not with us, we will not give them [any] of the spoil ... save to every man his wife and his children" (1 Sam. 30:22). David's just spirit was so incensed at such a suggestion that he laid down a rule that remained a statute for Israel throughout the days of the kingdom. He said, "The share of the man who stayed with the supplies is to be the same as that of him who went down to the battle. All will share alike" (1 Sam. 30:24, NIV). This was a noble and enlightened law and a principle still applicable in a congregation of Christians. Each one is expected to do only what he has the talents to do, and then each one will share equally God's grace.

When David reached Ziklag, he further showed his unselfish nature and political shrewdness by sending some of the spoil to the leaders of the Judean villages where he and his men ranged. He sent a message with the spoil: "A present for you of the spoil of the enemies of the Lord" (1 Sam. 30:26). Certainly this helped make the elders of God's people feel favorably disposed toward the leadership of David.

SAUL AND THE MEDIUM

After David left King Achish, the Philistines continued to gather themselves together at Shunem to invade Israel. Likewise, Saul gathered all of Israel's troops together and camped at Gilboa. "When Saul saw the host of Philistines, he was afraid, and his heart greatly trembled" (1 Sam. 28:5). Saul called for prophets and inquired of God concerning the impending battle, but God did not answer him by the Urim and Thummim. (This indicates that by this time there was more than one ephod with an Urim and Thummim. Whether this was by God's will or man's we don't know.) Saul then asked the Lord to answer him in a dream, but He did not.

Saul now grew desperate. There was no channel through which God answered man that Saul hadn't tried. So he decided to seek guidance through the Devil's channel, using a medium. But by official edict earlier in his reign, he had banished all those who communicated with the spirits. Now he commanded his servants, "Seek me a woman that hath a familiar spirit, that I may go to her, and inquire of her" (1 Sam. 28:7). The servants did not have to go looking, for they were familiar with one who lived at En-dor. Saul's edict against mediums was about as effective as edicts by governors and presidents today against drug pushers. Evil is pervasive and not easily legislated out of existence when it fills a need felt by a significant percentage of the population.

Saul disguised himself and went to this evil woman under the cover of darkness, but not even a starless night could hide the wickedness of Saul. "Divine unto me by the familiar spirit, and bring me him up," he requested of the medium (1 Sam. 28:8). The woman asked whom she should call up, and Saul said "Samuel." When Samuel actually appeared to the medium, she shrieked because she, of all people, was most surprised to see a real person coming up from the beyond. She then realized her client had deceived her and that he was King Saul, and she was terrified. Saul assured her, however, that no harm would befall her and that he desired

to continue the seance. The woman said, "I see
spirits ascending out of the earth." She described
an old man wrapped in a cloak, and Saul knew it
was Samuel. Bowing before him, he explained to
Samuel his dilemma and concluded with the plea,
"Make known unto me what I shall do" (1 Sam.
28:12-15).

The impatient, self-willed Saul was begging to be
told what to do, but it was too late! There is indeed
a sin unto death (1 John 5:16-17) that places one
beyond the mercy of our merciful God. The inspired
epithet given to Saul in 1 Chronicles 10:14 reads,
"[Saul] inquired not of the Lord: therefore he slew
him." Saul neglected God, and as one theologian
has well observed, "If we do not hear God's voice
when it goes well with us, God can and will refuse
to hear our voice when it goes ill with us."

Many today feel they can do without God's guidance until some overwhelming crisis arises, and then
God will hear and answer their prayer. But "how
shall we escape, if we neglect" the love and grace
God has offered us through Jesus (Heb. 2:3)? Fortu-
nately, God's concern for each person is so great
that this estranged position is not quickly reached.

Samuel did not answer Saul's question but rather
pronounced his doom.

Wherefore then dost thou ask of me, seeing the Lord
is departed from thee, and is become thine enemy?
. . . as he spake by me: for the Lord hath rent the
kingdom out of thine hand, and given it . . . to David:
because thou obeyedst not the voice of the Lord, nor
executedst his fierce wrath upon Amalek. . . . More-
over the Lord will also deliver Israel with thee into
the hand of the Philistines: and tomorrow shall thou
and thy sons be with me: the Lord also shall deliver

the host of Israel into the hand of the Philistines.
Then Saul fell straightway all along on the earth, and
was sore afraid, because of the words of Samuel.
(1 Sam. 28:16-20)[2]

THE END OF SAUL

The battle began, "and the men of Israel fled from
before the Philistines" (1 Sam. 31:1). The morale of
the men reflected the despondency of their commander. The battle turned into a rout, and, in the
disorderly flight, the Philistines closed in on Saul
and his sons. The sons, including Jonathan, were
killed, and the Philistine archers were harassing
Saul. He was shot and wounded. Then, in fear of
being made sport of as well as being killed by his
bitter enemies, Saul called on his armor-bearer to
kill him by thrusting him through with the sword.
Jewish tradition identifies the armor-bearer as the
wicked Doeg, who slaughtered the priests at Nob.
When the armor-bearer refused to kill him, Saul
killed himself. He had long ago committed spiritual
suicide, and now physical suicide. The armor-bearer,
seeing his king was dead, "fell likewise upon his
sword and died with him" (1 Sam. 31:5).

Not only did the soldiers of Israel flee the battle-
ground, but the protectors of Israel's fortified cities
also fled, leaving Israel defenseless. Therefore, along
with Saul fell not only his sons, but all of northern
Israel. "The Philistines came and dwelt in the cities"
(1 Sam. 31:7).

On the day after the battle, the Philistines came
to strip the slain, including Saul. They took Saul's
armor which they put in the house of their idol

gods, and they cut off his head which they fastened to the house of Dagon, the chief of their false gods.

Whenever God's people allow victory to the heathen, it brings reproach upon the name of Jehovah. He will not allow His people to lose except when they turn from His way. Today Christians can bring deep reproach to the precious name of Christ by not following His way. We are told to put on the "whole armor of God, that ye may be able to withstand the evil day" (Eph. 6:13). The citizens of Christ's kingdom today face enemies far more wicked than the Philistines.

Hearing of Saul's death, the valiant men of the trans-Jordan city of Jabesh-gilead crossed Philistine territory and took the bodies of Saul and his sons down from the wall where they were hanging. They returned to Jabesh-gilead with the bodies, and after burning them they buried the bones under a tree. Years later, King David collected the bones of Saul and Jonathan and took them into the territory of Benjamin. He gave them a proper burial in the tomb of Kish, Saul's father (2 Sam. 21:12-14).

This dangerous mission was undertaken by the men of Jabesh-gilead in thankful remembrance of the time when Saul delivered them from the Ammonites. Saul had just been chosen by lot to be the first king of Israel (1 Sam. 10), and he was not well accepted by all the people, having not proved himself. He received word that Nahash the Ammonite was threatening to put out the right eye of every man in Jabesh-gilead, and to make them his servants as a reproach upon all Israel. When Saul heard this, "the Spirit of God came upon Saul" (1 Sam. 11:6), and he raised an army that defeated the Ammonites at Jabesh-gilead. After that first victory, Saul was fully accepted as king of all Israel. What a wonderful beginning Saul had to end so shamefully! "So Saul died for his transgression which he committed against the Lord, even against the word of the Lord, which he kept not" (1 Chron. 10:13).

DAVID'S REACTION

David had been back in Ziklag only three days when the news of the death of Saul reached him. An Amalekite was scavenging immediately after the battle at Gilboa when he came across the body of King Saul. He removed the crown and bracelet from the corpse and headed south toward Ziklag to present them to David, fully expecting a great reward. He rent his clothes and put dirt on his head to show mourning. When he reached David, he fell to the earth, did obeisance, and told David that Saul and Jonathan were dead and the battle was lost. He presented the crown and bracelet to David, telling a false version of the death of Saul, one he felt would present him in a favorable light to David. He said,

> As I happened by chance upon mount Gilboa, behold, Saul leaned upon his spear; and, lo, the chariots and horsemen followed hard after him. And when he looked behind him, he saw me, and called unto me. And I answered, Here am I. And he said unto me, Who art thou? And I answered him, I am an Amalekite. He said unto me again, Stand, I pray thee, upon me, and slay me: for anguish is come upon me, because my life is yet whole in me. So I stood upon him, and slew him, because I was sure that he could not live after that he was fallen: and I took the crown

that was upon his head, and the bracelet that was
on his arm, and have brought them hither unto my
lord. (2 Sam. 1:6-10)

David's first reaction to the sad news was to
mourn the fall of Saul, Jonathan, and the people of
Jehovah. A little later he passed swift judgment on
the Amalekite. He said to him, "Thy blood be upon
thy head; for thy mouth hath testified against thee,
saying, I have slain the Lord's anointed" (2 Sam.
1:16). Then David had him executed on the spot.

David composed a lamentation for Saul and
Jonathan entitled "The Song of the Bow" which was
written in the book of Vasher and incorporated in
the first chapter of 2 Samuel.[3] In this lamentation,
"the bow of Jonathan" is mentioned in verse 22.
David may well have remembered the arrows shot
by Jonathan to signal him to leave the presence of
Saul. The love shared by David and Jonathan is
commemorated in verses 25 and 26.

"How are the mighty fallen" is the theme of the
song, repeated three times to emphasize the point
that even the mightiest fall, good and bad alike. No
one lives forever. "It is appointed unto men once
to die" (Heb. 9:27). Change is inevitable, and David
had waited patiently for the crown. Now the waiting
was over.

The Psalms of David's Early Life

Of the eighteen psalms ascribed to David prior to
his being anointed king of Judah, most were written
during his flight from Saul. The outstanding theme
is praise to God. David repeatedly expressed his trust

in God. We have already considered fourteen of these psalms. The other four are as follows:

Psalm 12 begins with the universal cry of the upright, which is, "Help, Lord." David feared, as so many have before and after him, that faithful, righteous men were going to cease to exist because the wickedness of the world was so pervasive. But he expressed his faith in God's protective care. He also contrasted the loose and empty words of humanity to the pure and precious words of God.

David was being unmercifully hunted by Saul when he wrote Psalm 13, so four times in this short song he cried out, "How long?"

Psalm 17 was yet another prayer for the Lord's protection against evil oppressors who are satisfied in the riches of this world. David sought more than this life can give. He would only be satisfied when "I will behold thy face in righteousness" and "when I awake, with thy likeness" (v. 15). He believed, as did Job (Job 19:26-27), that he would see his Lord face to face in a life after this one. Like the apostle John (1 John 3:2), David didn't know what form he would have, but he knew he would be in the likeness of the Lord.

While David was in the wilderness of Judah, he wrote in Psalm 63, "O God, you are my God, earnestly I seek you; my soul thirsts for you . . . in a dry and weary land where there is no water" (v. 1, NIV). In this touching psalm of praise, we can see why God loved David so much. David told his Lord that His lovingkindness was better than life itself, and that he would praise Him with joyful lips as long as he lived. David wrote that he even laid awake at night thinking of how much the Lord had helped him, saying, "My soul followeth hard after thee" (v. 8).

Putting Truth into Action

1. At what point did Saul pass the point of no return in his spiritual decline? When are people today in danger of passing that point?
2. How should we apply in our congregations David's rule that all God's "warriors" should share equally the "spoils of victory?"
3. Why, when God has provided many good ways for us to know His will, do people, still resort to astrology and necromancy?
4. Compare the Saul of the Old Testament to the Saul of the New Testament.

CHAPTER 5

A New Beginning

2 Samuel 2 through 5
1 Chronicles 14

Have you noticed how God seems to specialize in new beginnings? After Job was tested, for example, God gave him more possessions and a larger family than before, and he lived to see four generations of his descendants. Consider the apostle Paul, who before his encounter with the risen Jesus on the Damascus road was a chief persecutor of His people. But after his new beginning, he became perhaps the greatest Christian missionary ever, as well as the inspired writer of much of the New Testament.

David also experienced a new beginning after the death of Saul, and from this stage of his life we gain the assurance that if we persevere faithfully in trials, as David did, we, too, will see, in God's perfect time, a new beginning and the fulfillment of His promises.

As the third decade of David's life changed into the fourth, a dramatic change occurred in his status. The outlaw became a victorious king.

With Saul dead, David asked God if the time had arrived for him to come out of exile and go up into Judah. Jehovah told him to go to Hebron, the ancestral city of Abraham, where Abraham had buried his wife Sarah (Gen. 23:19). So David, his men, and

their families moved north and settled in Hebron.
Jehovah had led and blessed Abraham. David was
led by Jehovah and surely would also be blessed.
Such must have been the thinking of the elders of
the large and powerful tribe of Judah. Therefore, "the
men of Judah came, and there they anointed David
king over the house of Judah" (2 Sam. 2:4).

When Samuel had anointed David ten long years
before, it had been "in promise," but now it was in
reality so far as the tribe of Judah was concerned.
In the sunlit hills of Judah, just twenty-five miles
south of the city David would make the abiding
capital of the kingdom of Israel, Jerusalem, David
broke out his harp in joy and sang, "The Lord is
my light and my salvation; whom shall I fear? . . . One
thing have I desired of the Lord, that I will seek
after; that I may dwell in the house of the Lord all
the days of my life, to behold the beauty of the Lord,
and to inquire in his temple" (Psa. 27:1, 4).[1]

Psalm 27 has been called a "composite" psalm
because it divides into two parts that sharply con-
trast in their mood. The first part (vv. 1-6) is joyous
and confident, while the second part (vv. 7-14) is
contemplative and even sad. Properly considered,
the two parts complement each other and conform
to David's manner of suddenly changing the spirit
of his psalms. Generally, his psalms switch from a
petition for help to a hymn of thanks; from somber-
ness to radiance. Here in Psalm 27 the order is
reversed. However, that seems natural if this psalm
were written before he was anointed king, as the title
states in both the Septuagint and the Vulgate. One
can easily envision the joy David felt at being asked
by the leaders of Judah to serve as their king. The
long-awaited opportunity was at last at hand, but

then came the sobering thought of the responsibilities the throne would bring. He would need more help, guidance, deliverance, and patience in the years to come than ever he had needed in the past. No wonder, then, that the second part of this coronation psalm is less joyous than the first.

In verse 9, David remembered Saul and how Jehovah had removed His Spirit from him and had hidden His face from him. David prayed, "Put not thy servant away in anger," because he remembered what God had said: "Seek ye my face." David's heart replied, "Thy face, Lord, will I seek" (v. 8). "Teach me thy way, O Lord," he continued. "Lead me in a plain [well-marked] path" (v. 11). "When my father and mother forsake me, then the Lord will take me up" (v. 10). "I [would have] fainted, unless I had believed to see the goodness of the Lord in the land of the living" (v. 13). Then in conclusion, David said to himself, "Wait on the Lord: be of good courage, and he shall strengthen thine heart" (v. 14).[2]

It is fitting that David's first recorded act as king of Judah was one of gentle thoughtfulness. The news came to him of the burial of Saul and Jonathan by the men of Jabesh-gilead, and David sent messengers to them, commending them for their brave and kind action. As king of Judah, he placed himself in their debt. Not only was this the proper thing for David to do, but it was also politically expedient.

Ish-bosheth Made King of Israel

While David was trying to win the allegiance of the northern and trans-Jordan tribes, Abner, Saul's general and uncle, was propping up a puppet king of his own making. After the rout of Israel's army and the death of Saul and his sons at Gilboa, Abner retreated across the Jordan and set up headquarters for his new government at Mahanaim in Gilead. (Mahanaim was named by the patriarch Jacob in honor of the host of God's angels who met him there as he returned from exile [Gen. 32:1-2].)

Second Samuel 2:10 says Ish-bosheth was forty years old when he began to reign. Thus, he must have been Saul's first son born shortly after Saul began his forty-year reign. Since there is no mention of him prior to this time, it may be assumed he was weak either physically, mentally, or both. Not being a warrior, he lived in the shadow of his younger brothers, especially Jonathan, and was listed fourth among the sons of Saul (1 Chron. 8:33; in this passage, Ish-bosheth is called Esh-baal).[3]

In 2 Samuel 2:10-11 are two time periods that are difficult for some to reconcile. The verses state that Ish-bosheth reigned over Israel for two years, but David reigned over Judah for seven and a half years at Hebron. The Bible, not being primarily a book of history, often does not furnish a detailed chronological record, giving only the more important facts. These two time periods are easily reconciled when we consider that David was made king of Judah shortly after Saul's death, while it undoubtedly took Abner an extended time to bring about the crowning of Ish-bosheth by the badly scattered and disheartened elders of the other eleven tribes. And after the assassination of Ish-bosheth, which we will soon study, there must have been another prolonged period of time before the eleventh tribes were sure David's hand was not involved in the murder and he should be crowned their king. These two periods before and after the short reign of Ish-bosheth could more than account for the five and a half years when Israel was without a king, whereas Judah was blessed with David as king the entire time.

ISRAEL DEFEATED BY JUDAH

Besides establishing Ish-bosheth as a puppet king, Abner also intended to crush the forces of David and extend his power over all twelve tribes. To achieve this, Abner moved his army, composed chiefly of Benjamites, across the Jordan to Gibeon, which was some twenty-six miles from Mahanaim, close to the border between Benjamin and Judah.

David in return sent an army under his cousin Joab northward from Hebron, also some twenty-six miles, to protect Judah's boundary. The two armies camped on opposite sides of the pool of Gibeon. Why didn't David, the warrior, go to defend Judah against Israel? In accordance with God's will and desiring to unite all twelve tribes under his rule, David could not afford to be involved in a battle that would pit brother against brother, tribe against tribe.

As the two armies faced each other, Abner proposed a deadly game to prepare the armies for battle. Each side was to choose twelve young men who would meet in mortal combat in an area between the two armies. The result of this deadly game was a bloody draw, for "they caught everyone his fellow by the head, and thrust his sword in his fellow's side; so they fell down together" (2 Sam. 2:16). Appropriately, the place was called "the field of blades." Young men have always been considered disposable in the games played by people of power.

Following the game, the two sides met in fierce battle. Abner lost 360 men, but Joab lost only 19 and gained a victory for Judah. Realizing he was defeated, Abner turned and ran. Asahel, the younger brother of Joab, chased him. Asahel was young and as fast as a deer, and he caught up with Abner. Twice Abner, the seasoned man of blood, warned Asahel to turn aside and engage a man his own age, but when he would not, Abner killed him (2 Sam. 2:23).

The Benjamites regrouped around Abner, and as the sun set on the first battle of what was to be a "long war between the house of Saul and the house of David" (2 Sam. 3:1), Abner called to Joab and requested that the battle be ended. In his request he asked a question that is as pertinent today as it was then: "Shall the sword devour for ever?" (2 Sam. 2:26). Joab broke off the pursuit, and Abner's retreating forces recrossed the Jordan. Joab and Abishai buried their younger brother Asahel at Bethlehem, rejoined their army, and returned to Hebron.

ABNER SWITCHES TO DAVID

David's power and fortune grew steadily stronger, while the remnant of Saul's kingdom became weaker and weaker. Abner became so overbearing that Ishbosheth protested, which incensed Abner and led him to change his allegiance, such as it was, from the house of Saul to the house of David. He boasted he would bring down the house of Saul and put David on the throne "over Israel and over Judah,

from Dan even to Beer-sheba" (2 Sam. 3:10).[4] He
would work to bring about what "the Lord hath
sworn to David" (2 Sam. 3:9). Abner was saying, in
effect, that he knew God had promised to make
David king over all twelve tribes, but he had worked
against God's will in the past. And though God had
not made David king of Israel without his help, *he*
would do it with a little help from God. Incredible
arrogance!

Abner really changed his allegiance because he
knew David was increasing in power, and he was
looking out after number one. He sent envoys to
David, saying, "Make an agreement with me, and I
will help you bring all Israel over to you" (2 Sam.
3:12, NIV). David replied that he would make an
agreement with Abner, but he would see him face
to face only after Abner had returned his first wife,
Michal, to him. Remember that Saul had given
Michal to another man after David fled Saul's court.
David did not underestimate Abner's ability to sway
Israel, but if he were to enter into league with him,
Abner must, from the beginning, do his bidding.

King David also sent the same demand to King
Ish-bosheth. Both Ish-bosheth and Abner did as
David ordered, and Michal, possibly against her
wishes, was returned to David despite the tears of
her second husband, who tried to follow but was
turned back. In the meanwhile, Abner spoke favorably in behalf of David to his tribe of Benjamin and
to the elders of the other ten tribes who were under
his influence. When he brought Michal to David,
he was ready to deal. David made a feast for Abner
and the men who were with him, and Abner promised to bring all Israel to David to proclaim him
king. Then David sent Abner away "in peace,"

which means he was granted safe conduct (2 Sam. 3:20-21).

The Bible gives no indication that, during the entire negotiations, David consulted with Jehovah. Was David assuming God was working through Abner? If so, he was assuming too much.

ABNER AND ISH-BOSHETH SLAIN

During the time Abner had been with David, Joab was away on a raiding foray. Had David sent him away on purpose, knowing bad blood existed between Joab and Abner? Regardless, shortly after Abner left, Joab returned to Hebron, bringing in great spoil, and was greeted with the news of Abner's visit. He immediately went to see David and in an agitated voice demanded, "What hast thou done? . . . Why is it that thou hast sent him away?" (2 Sam. 3:24). He assured David that Abner had visited only to deceive him and spy on him. Then, after he left David, he sent messengers after Abner with instructions to bring him back. When Abner returned, Joab quickly disposed of him, getting revenge for the death of Asahel.

Joab's action placed David's possession of the crown of Israel in jeopardy. "When David heard it, he said, I and my kingdom are guiltless before the Lord for ever from the blood of Abner the son of Ner: Let it rest on the head of Joab, and on all his father's house" (2 Sam. 3:28-29). David then ordered everyone, including Joab, to fully enter into mourning for Abner. Abner was buried in Hebron with full honors, and David's personal part in the burial and mourning convinced all Israel that he had no hand in his murder. Although David was weakened by the action of Joab and he placed a curse upon Joab and his family, David did not punish him.

Joab continued to play a prominent part throughout the life of David. He was the only individual who could override David's decisions and get by with it. Why did he repeatedly do this, and why did David allow him to do so? Another key question is whether Joab acted because he thought it best for David or because he was only looking out for himself. He is an enigma, and you can make your own guess about his basic motivation.

King Ish-bosheth was dismayed when he received the news of Abner's assassination, not knowing his own assassination was imminent. Later—apparently soon after Abner's death—he was taking his noon nap when two of his captains, men of the tribe of Benjamin named Baanah and Rechab, crept into his house. They found his room, struck him dead, cut off his head, and escaped with it, traveling through the night to get to Hebron and present the head to David. They were certain, just like the Amalekite who brought Saul's crown to David, that he would reward them handsomely. But much to their chagrin, David reacted angrily, calling them wicked men and ordering their execution that the earth might be rid of them (2 Sam. 4:9-12). He also ordered that the severed hands and feet of the assassins be hung in a public place as a warning to others of the swift justice awaiting criminals.

DAVID ANOINTED KING OF ISRAEL AND JUDAH

Without the modern means of instant communication that we enjoy, months and years passed before "all the tribes of Israel" came together to David at Hebron to make him king over the twelve tribes united (2 Sam. 5:1-3). According to 1 Chronicles 12:23-40, there were 340,800 men gathered at Hebron representing every tribe, and they were "of one heart" (v. 38). Is it any wonder that David wrote, "Behold, how good and how pleasant it is for brethren to dwell together in unity!" (Psa. 133:1)? David had first been anointed by Samuel, then by the elders of the tribe of Judah, and finally by the elders of all Israel.[5]

At his third anointing, David in Psalm 133 compared the blessedness of the unity of all Israel to the precious oil (the Spirit of God) that was poured upon the head of Aaron when he was anointed as the first high priest. He also compared the preciousness of unity to God's anointing the earth with dew. David gave God's anointing of the earth a double meaning: (1) the physical blessings God has shown to His creation, and (2) the spiritual grace poured out at Zion upon us by Christ, the Anointed One. It is by His blood that we are cleansed from sin and granted "the blessing, even life for evermore" (v. 3). Thus, we, by obedience to the good news, are anointed and become the chosen of God.

For three days the great host of Israel held a feast to honor David. The food provided was meal and flour for breads, olive oil for cooking, wine for drinking, pressed cakes of raisins and figs, and beef and mutton for meats. It may not have been a fancy menu, according to our tastes, but it was wholesomely filling.

Following the feast, "king David made a league (covenant) with them (the elders of Israel) in Hebron before the Lord" (2 Sam. 5:3). Therefore, David was not an absolute monarch but was bound by this agreement. We don't know what was contained in the covenant, but in Psalm 101 he listed the principles that would guide him as king; these may reflect items in the agreement.

In the eight verses of Psalms 101 David lists eight principles as follows: (1) I will sing praises unto Jehovah. (2) I will behave wisely in Jehovah's perfect way and will walk in the integrity of my heart. (3) I will set no base goal. I detest those who swerve from the perfect (straight) way. Their evil will not become a part of me. (4) I will not be perverse of heart or place my trust in any evil person. (5) I will not tolerate those who slander their neighbors and think too highly of themselves. (6) I will shepherd those who faithfully follow the straight way. (7) I will not tolerate those who practice deceit. (8) I will daily judge the people that justice may be done. These are excellent principles for a president or prime minister to follow today.

In 2 Samuel 5:2 we find the first use of the concept of shepherding to describe the duties of a king. A shepherd did not own the sheep, but they were entrusted to his leadership. A king was to lead his people as an agent of God, not as their master (owner). David's fidelity in shepherding his father's sheep had trained him to shepherd God's people as a king. He understood that a king was to lead, not drive, his people, to protect, not oppress them, and to provide for them. David was following in good footsteps, for Jacob, the prince of God, had been a shepherd, and Moses, the great savior of the Israelites, had also been a shepherd. Likewise, the leaders of the Lord's church in the local congregations are compared to shepherds in the New Testament (Acts 20:28-30; 1 Pet. 5:2).

Finally, after seven and a half years as king of Judah at Hebron, the patience of David was rewarded. Now, in God's good time, David became king over all Israel. He was approximately thirty-seven years old, and it would be almost one thousand fifty years before "in the fullness of time" the divine son of David would be born.

JERUSALEM

One of the first things David realized as king of all Israel was the need for a new capital, one not connected with a particular tribe. He wanted a capital that could be the center of Israel's religious activities, the city of Jehovah, and also the center of their national life. He selected a city located on the border line between Judah and Benjamin. It was on a plateau, crowned by a cluster of hills, the highest of which was topped by a rock citadel.[6]

The only problem with the city was that it was inhabited by the Jebusites, one of the original Canaanite tribes. They felt so secure in their citadel that they boasted that even the lame and blind could defeat any army David might hurl against them. But David knew a secret. Steps had been laboriously chiselled out of a natural crevice in the stone of the hill down to the cool, clear water of the spring Gihon. The steps formed a vertical tunnel into the heart of the citadel. David issued a challenge: "Whosoever getteth up to the gutter, and smiteth the Jebusites, he shall be chief and captain" (2 Sam. 5:8; 1 Chron. 11:6). Joab went first, again displaying his bold courage. The city was captured, and David took the stronghold of Zion and called it the city of David.[7] He built up the city, and Joab made repairs (2 Sam. 5:7, 9; 1 Chron. 11:7-8).

The city David conquered was ancient even in his day. It was first mentioned in Genesis 14:18 as the city of Melchizedek, "king of Salem . . . priest of the most high God." *Salem* means "peace" (Heb. 7:2), and by adding *Jeru,* which means "city of God," to it, Jerusalem became the city of the God of peace. Indeed, Jehovah is the God of peace, but His chosen city has seen little peace during the centuries, continuing to this day. It has been repeatedly besieged. Its walls have been leveled. It has been divided, conquered, and razed.

DAVID WAXED GREATER AND GREATER

As David waxed greater and greater (2 Sam. 5:10), there were two opposite reactions from Israel's neighboring states. Hiram, king of Tyre, established a friendly and helpful relationship with Israel that would continue through the reign of Solomon. Tyre (meaning "rocky"), the most noted of the Phoenician cities, traded skilled craftsmen, sailing vessels, and cedar from the forests of Lebanon, which were all needed by both David and Solomon in their ambitious building programs, for the agricultural produce of Israel.

On the other hand, the kings of the Philistines decided to try to crush David before Israel became stronger. As they gathered their armies, David inquired of Jehovah, "Wilt thou deliver them into mine hand?" (2 Sam. 5:19). God replied in the affirmative, David marched his army against the ancient enemy, and the Philistines' defeat turned into a rout.

Many images of their gods were left behind by the Philistines as they fled and were taken by David's men. This embarrassment to the Philistines and their gods may have reminded David that this same enemy had taken the sacred Ark of the Covenant from the Israelites in the previous century. It had been captured in the days of the wicked sons of Eli (1 Sam. 4). However, Jehovah plagued the Philistines and caused them to rid themselves of His Ark, but it had never been restored to its rightful place in the most holy place of the tabernacle. It was in the house of Abinadab in Kirjath-jearim (1 Sam. 7:1), which was in the border area still heavily patrolled by the Philistines. David may have determined to restore the Ark if the Lord allowed him to free the land from the control of the Philistines.

After their defeat, the Philistines regrouped, strengthened themselves, and descended once more upon David. It was, in substance, still David versus Goliath, or the new kid on the block versus the establishment. When David inquired of God about this second battle, he was told to circle around and prepare to attack the enemy from behind.

He was to gather his forces under cover of a grove of trees. Various Bible translations identify the kind of trees differently; the King James, for example, calls them mulberry trees, whereas the New International Version says balsam trees. In our efforts to identify the trees, we may well lose the inspiring lesson to be found in the passage, which is what God did.

God said, "As soon as you hear the sound of marching in the tops of the balsam trees, move quickly, because that will mean the Lord has gone out in front of you to strike the Philistine army" (2 Sam. 5:24, NIV). This wasn't simply a signal to attack caused by a wind's rustling the treetops. It was the sound of God's innumerable legions of angelic warriors preceding David's army into battle.

The Lord is no onlooker but an ally to His chosen people. Divine assistance is not meant to replace our utmost effort (Phil. 2:12), but to quicken it. "Without me ye can do nothing," said Jesus (John 15:5), but with Him nothing is impossible (Luke 18:27). Evil is mighty, but good is almighty.

The battle was a decisive victory for God's people, and Israel was secure. Now David's task would be to unify, strengthen, and expand his kingdom.[8]

"The fame of David went out into all lands; and the Lord brought the fear of him upon all nations" (1 Chron. 14:17). And in Psalm 18, written about this time, David declared his love for God and reliance upon Him as his shield and refuge (vv. 1-2). In telling God he loved Him he used the verb denoting the tenderest affection. This verb is used nowhere else in the Bible to refer to a person's love of God, but is reserved to describe God's love for us. The verse using this verb is excluded—maybe because it was too personal—from the version of the psalm given in 2 Samuel 22, which was, it seems, prepared for use in public services.

Notice that David used seven titles for God: my strength, my rock, my fortress, my deliverer, my shield, the horn of my salvation, and my high tower. The mystic number seven symbolized perfection in sacred writings. This was David's longest psalm and his most polished and reflective one. In it we do not find the abrupt thought transitions so typical of David's other psalms.

In verses 4-18, David recounted how Jehovah moved heaven and earth when David called on Him for deliverance. God delivered David "because he delighted in me" (v. 19). Why did God delight in David? "The Lord rewarded me according to my righteousness. . . . For I have kept the ways of the Lord. . . . I did not put away his statutes for me" (vv. 20-22).

In accordance with God's relationship to him, David stated in verses 25-27 the grand principle that God deals with every person just as that person is. If a person is merciful, God will be merciful to him. If a person is pure, God will show Himself pure. But if a person is perverse, God will condemn him. God will not be evil to the evil, but He will punish their evilness. Isn't this principle the basis of Christ's Beatitudes? It's a basic rule of life: we reap what we sow.

David returned in verses 28-50 to ascribing praise and thanksgiving to the almighty Lord for His blessings. In verse 35, he ascribed a quality to God found nowhere else in the Bible: "Thy *gentleness* hath made me great" (emphasis added). David had faced some harrowing trials and temptations in his period of preparation, but as king, looking back, he saw that his Lord had lifted him from the sheepfold to the throne with a gentle hand. Every person reaching the maturity of his life may look back and find that the Lord has either been a gentle or stern father in accordance with the individual's submissiveness to God's will.

Some commentators see a messianic reference in the closing verse, which reads: "to David, and to his seed for evermore." Actually, the entire psalm is secondarily applicable to Christ as shown by its use in the New Testament. Verses 2 and 49 are both sources for the words of Christ (Heb. 2:13; Rom. 15:9).

Putting Truth into Action

1. What qualities of David's, as he assumed the throne of a united Israel, are most worth pursuing today?
2. David clearly believed the swift, severe, and public punishment of murderers would deter others from committing the crime. Is this a valid perspective today? Why or why not?
3. What does it mean to shepherd someone spiritually? What are the advantages of having a spiritual shepherd? What are some potential dangers?
4. Abner and Joab were ancient "power brokers." Discuss the roles of modern power brokers.

CHAPTER 6

Learning to Worship

2 Samuel 6
1 Chronicles 13 through 16

Suppose a man needs to repair the wiring in an electrical outlet in his bathroom, and there's a puddle of water on the floor in front of the outlet—but the man doesn't know the danger of standing in water while working with electricity. He isn't foolish and has no wish to commit suicide—he just doesn't know. If he stands in the water and comes into contact with electricity, is his ignorance going to protect him from shock? No.

The same principle is true in almost every case: ignorance exposes us to danger. We aren't protected from natural laws (like those that govern electricity), man-made laws, or God's laws by being unfamiliar with them. And if we want to please God, we need to have not only good intentions (important as they are), but also knowledge of how He wants us to worship Him.

David learned some important and painful lessons about worship when he tried to bring the Ark of the Covenant into his new capital city. Through his experiences and the psalms he wrote at the time, we also can learn much about the proper worship of our Lord.

THE ARK BROUGHT TO JERUSALEM

In about 1042 B.C., when David was approximately forty-three, he called an assembly of the leaders of Israel, "the captains of thousands and hundreds" (1 Chron. 13:1). This pattern of leadership dated back to the advice given to Moses about the delegation of authority by his father-in-law, Jethro (Exod. 18:13-26). David suggested to the assembly that the Ark, which had been languishing in obscurity since before the time of Saul, be brought up to Jerusalem. The assembly approved.

We don't know whether the leaders realized the presence of the Ark of God in Jerusalem would make that city the religious as well as political center of all Israel. Certainly God and David knew. The tabernacle had been moved to Gibeon, probably by Saul (1 Chron. 16:39), but David, rather than moving it again, prepared a new tabernacle for the Ark in Jerusalem. He would later purpose to build in Jerusalem a great temple, patterned after the tabernacle, to house the Ark of Jehovah.[1]

To bring the Ark from Kirjath-jearim to Jerusalem, a sturdy, new cart was built. David and a host from all Israel rejoiced with great enthusiasm as the Ark was taken from Abinadab's house, placed on the new cart, and pulled by a select team of oxen. Uzza and Ahio, sons or most likely grandsons of Abinadab, were given the honor and responsibility of driving the oxen. However, the road was not a smooth highway, and the cart lacked shock absorbers, so it wasn't long before the Ark appeared to be in danger of falling off the cart. When Uzza reached out to hold the Ark, "the anger of the Lord was kindled against Uzza, and he smote him, because he put his

hand to the ark: and there he died before God"
(1 Chron. 13:10).

What had started out so joyfully ended quickly
in tragedy. The Ark was carried into the house of
Obed-edom, the crowd was dispersed, and David
was "displeased." He was a man perplexed, vexed,
and angry at God. He didn't know why Jehovah's
wrath broke forth on Uzza but he knew that something far larger than Uzza's touching the Ark was
involved.

God had rained on David's parade, and David was
at first angry at God. Then he began to feel fear, and
he was "afraid of God" (1 Chron. 13:12). In his fear
he joined good company with the biblical host of
the righteous. Adam was the first to learn to be
afraid of God (Gen. 3:10). Jacob was afraid when he
realized the omnipresence of God (Gen. 28:17), and
Peter was afraid in the presence of the Master (Luke
5:8). Saul, later known as Paul, thought he was
righteous but became afraid when the True Light
appeared to him (Acts 9:3-5). Later he said, "Knowing therefore the terror of the Lord, we persuade
men?" (2 Cor. 5:11). Solomon wrote an inspired
commandment: "Fear God, and keep his commandments: for this is the whole duty of man" (Eccles.
12:13).

There is definitely a positive role for fear in our
lives. It makes us cautious, it prevents us from
becoming overconfident, and it often may save our
lives physically and spiritually. Everyone needs to
know and experience the love, approval, and care
of God. Everyone also needs to know and experience
the fear of God. One gives us assurance; the other
gives us humility and reverence.

David's anger turned into embarrassment, and he smarted from it but did not foolishly accuse the Lord as some have done. Rather he asked, "How shall I bring the ark of God home to me?" (1 Chron. 13:12). A search of the law was made, and a passage was found telling exactly how the Ark was to be transported (Num. 4:1-15). The correct method of transportation was for the priests to first cover the Ark and then place carrying poles through the rings attached to its corners. Then the Levites of the family of Kohath would carry the Ark on their shoulders, but they could not touch it.

David realized an error had been made in attempting to move the Ark on a cart. Speaking to the Levites, he said, "Because ye did it not at the first, the Lord our God made a breach upon us, for that we sought him not after the due order" (1 Chron. 15:13).

Two important lessons are highlighted at the beginning of this chapter and can be confirmed from other Scriptures which are to be found in this incident: (1) ignorance of God's word is no excuse, and (2) good intent never excuses wrongdoing.

A word must be said here concerning David's attempt to transport the Ark of God on a cart. More than a generation had passed since the Israelites had transported it, so experiential knowledge was not available. It was in the scrolls of the law of God given through Moses, but how common were copies of these scrolls among a highly illiterate people? The priests should have known, but Saul had had almost all of them killed. Before the first attempt to move the Ark, David should have had the subject researched, as he did before the successful second effort. However, he admitted his error and corrected it. Far too many individuals refuse to admit their mistakes.

Three months passed, and David again called Israel together to bring the Ark the rest of the way to Jerusalem. In the intervening time, "the Lord blessed the house of Obed-edom, and all that he had" (1 Chron. 13:14). The Targums[2] say that Obed-edom's wife and each of his eight daughters-in-law conceived, "and each brought forth eight at one birth, fourscore and one." As Adam Clarke said, commenting on this probable overstatement, "All rabbis must be allowed to deal in the marvelous."

In preparation for moving of the Ark, the priests and Levites underwent the ceremonies of sanctification as prescribed in the law of Moses. The day arrived, and David dressed, not in his kingly garments, but like the Levites, in a robe of fine linen and an ephod of linen. When he saw that "God helped the Levites that bare the ark of the covenant of the Lord" (1 Chron. 15:26), abundant sacrifices were made. David was so filled with joy that he leaped and danced to the music as the parade moved into Jerusalem.

The Ark was set in the tent David had pitched for it, and David offered a burnt offering and peace offerings. He blessed the people in the name of Jehovah and gave to every man and woman a loaf of bread, a piece of meat, and flagon of wine. Then the people went home (2 Sam. 6:17-19).

David also went home to bless his household and to share with them his great joy and triumph. Michal came out to meet him, not to congratulate her husband but to condemn him. From a window she had watched the procession pass the palace. She had seen David leaping and whirling in his simple linen garment, and "she despised him in her heart" (2 Sam. 6:16). She said sarcastically, "How glorious was the king of Israel today, who uncovered himself today in the eyes of the handmaids of his servants, as one of the vain fellows shamelessly uncovereth himself!" (2 Sam. 6:20).

David, taken by surprise by this bitter attack on his personal conduct, slashed back, saying he had celebrated before the Lord, and the Lord had made him ruler over His people rather than her father or anyone from his family. Apparently as a result of her attack on David, the Bible says that "Michal the daughter of Saul had no child unto the day of her death" (2 Sam. 6:23).

What made the woman who had once loved David turn to despising him? Earlier she had delivered him from her father's wrath, but now she accused him of vulgar behavior. This incident typical of many marriages that begin in mutual love and slide into alienation. Governments, technology, and the environment change with the centuries, but human nature has remained the same from the beginning. A number of commentaries consulted on this incident state that Michal had changed over the years, growing regal, aloof, and irreligious. This, they explain, is why she couldn't tolerate David's common touch or religious fervor.

But then, all the commentators were men. Not one wondered if her attitude were a reaction to David's forcibly taking her from her second husband. She had not been asked if she wished to be reunited with David. Also, not one commentator wondered what she had suffered as David took more and more wives over the years.

PSALMS CELEBRATING THE ARK

There are several psalms connected with the bringing of the Ark into Jerusalem. The most obvious is embedded in the narrative in 1 Chronicles 16:8-36. This official psalm was composed from parts of four other psalms. The first fifteen verses are from Psalm 105:1-15. The next eleven verses 23-33 are from Psalm 96:1-13. Verse 34 was a favorite expression of David's and is practically identical to the first verse of 106, 118, and 136. Verses 35-36 are found also in Psalm 106:47-48.

This psalm of thanksgiving divides into two parts: in verses 8-22, the people of Israel are thankful because they remember the divine care that had covered them from Abraham to the conquest of the promised land. In the second part, verses 23-36, all nations, even the entire universe, join in the praise of Jehovah, the God of Israel, until "he cometh to judge the earth" (v. 33).[3] The joy of praise must come from the pure heart that looks forward to judgment.

Standing out as the central diamond in this sparkling song of praise is verse 29: "Give unto the Lord the glory due unto his name: bring an offering, and come before him: worship the Lord in the beauty of holiness." David used this gem also in Psalm 96:8-9 and Psalm 29:2. When we think of our Creator, praise should well up in our hearts. To rob God of the praise due Him is indeed sinful.

There are two conditions listed as being necessary when we worship God: (1) Bring an offering when you come before Him. Don't come empty-handed as the one-talent man did. It's true that God needs nothing we can give, since all is His; but it's also true that He knew about and was pleased with the two mites the poor widow gave as she came before Him. He has given us of His grace so freely! What offering of praise and gratitude do we return? (2) We should worship Him "in the beauty of holiness." Some have explained this phrase as meaning "holiday attire" or "clothing suited to holy service." Certainly our sense of reverence will cause us to dress properly when we gather to worship, but David was speaking of the spiritual dress written of in Psalm 132:9 and 1 Peter 3:3-4. In preparation for worshiping Him, we should clothe ourselves with meekness, humility, reverence, sincerity, and purity.[4]

This psalm of David was entrusted to the chief singer or musician, Asaph. Asaph not only put David's psalms to music, but also composed some of the psalms in the Bible's inspired collection.

Of the three other psalms connected with the bringing of the Ark into Jerusalem, Psalm 24 also stands out. It was composed by David for the occasion and was sung (chanted antiphonally) by the great chorus as the Ark was being carried in. How grand is the opening verse: "The earth is the Lord's and the fullness thereof; the world, and they that dwell therein."

How solemn is the question: "Who shall ascend into the hill of the Lord? Or who shall stand in his holy place?" (v. 3).

How definitive is the answer: "He that hath clean hands, and a pure heart; who hath not lifted up his soul unto vanity, nor sworn deceitfully?" (v. 4).

How sure is the blessing: "He shall receive the blessing from the Lord, and righteousness from the God of his salvation" (v. 5).

How stirring is the order: "Lift up your heads, O ye gates; even lift them up, ye everlasting doors; and the King of glory shall come in" (v. 9).

How messianic is the description of the King: "Who is this King of glory? The Lord of hosts, he is the King of glory" (v. 10).[5]

Psalm 15 is an elaboration of Psalm 24:3. It's a description of the ideal citizen of Zion. The qualities of goodness do not change, so the description remains appropriate for us today. What manner of person does God want as a citizen of His kingdom? The answer is partly found in verses 2 and 3: a person who both does and says what is right and true and does not do or say what is evil or slanderous. This righteous citizen's attitude toward his fellow man is discussed in verse 4. He is to honor all who fear God but despise all vile men. His personal integrity causes him to keep his word even if it turns harmful to him. He will not use his money to extract usury from a needy man, nor will he accept money to pervert justice against an innocent man (v. 5).

The conclusion reached by the psalm is that such a man "shall never be moved." As Solomon said, "The righteous is an everlasting foundation" (Prov. 10:25). Such a person is a landmark rock to the righteous (1 Cor. 3:11). Wisely do the righteous sing:

> How firm a foundation ye saints of the Lord,
> Is laid for your faith in His excellent word!
> What more can He say than to you He has said,
> You who unto Jesus for refuge have fled?

"Fear not, I am with thee, O be not dismayed;
I, I am thy God, and will still give thee aid;
I'll strengthen thee, help thee, and cause thee to stand,
Upheld by My gracious omnipotent hand."

—George Keith

The third psalm connected to the bringing of the Ark of God into Jerusalem, Psalm 68, was a favorite of both the Huguenots and of Savanarola, the 15th century reformer. It is a song of praise to an almighty God who cares for those who are often neglected. It states that he is "a father to the fatherless, a defender of widows"; that he "led captives in His train" and "leads forth the prisoners with singing"; and that he "sets the lonely in families" and "provided for the poor." It declares, "Blessed be the Lord, who daily loadeth us with benefits, even the God of our salvation" (KJV). Such is the God we worship.

The relationship of this psalm to the historical occasion under discussion is found primarily in verses 24 through 27:

"Your procession has come into view, O God,
    the procession of my God and King into the sanctuary.
In front are the singers, after them the musicians;
    with them are the maidens playing tambourines,
Praise God in the great congregation;
    praise the Lord in the assembly of Israel."

With the Ark of God safely enshrined in a tabernacle in Jerusalem, there were now two holy places of worship in Israel: Jerusalem and Gibeon, where the original tabernacle with the great altar of burnt offering was located. Zadok, of the line of Eleazar, the son of Aaron (Exodus 6:23), was high priest at Gibeon while Ahimelech of the line of Ithamar, the

son of Aaron (1 Chron. 6:3), was high priest at
Jerusalem. Thus was begun the dual priesthood
which sometimes causes concern to the casual reader
of the New Testament, when one verse calls one
person by the title of high priest and another verse
gives the title to a different person. There seemed
to have been no schism between the two high priests,
for later we will find that both Zadok and Ahimelech
moved Judah to return David to the throne after
Absalom's insurrection.

David, at this time, reorganized the priests into
twenty-four groups or courses; sixteen of which
were of Eleazar and eight of Ithamar. This organization continued down into New Testament times, and
the head of each "course" was a chief priest and
formed a part of the Sanhedrin court. (Note that
Luke 1:5 refers to "of the course of Abijah.")

THE MIGHTY MEN OF DAVID

David's great organizational ability is not only
seen in his division of duties and responsibilities
of the priests and Levites but in every phase of his
administration (2 Sam. 8:15-18; 1 Chron. 18:14-17).
If it were not so tedious, we could study in depth
the organization of his military from the renowned
Gibborim or Mighty Men on down. These men are
recorded in 1 Chronicles 11:10-12 and 2 Samuel
23:8-39. The "Mighty Men" came to David before
he became mighty and they formed the core leadership of his army and guards throughout his life.
These men loved David and were intensely loyal to
him. Their devotion to him and his emotional response to it are illustrated in the scripture by the

following incident that took place at some time before the Philistines were completely subdued. David was in some sort of stronghold, and a garrison of Philistines was in Bethlehem. David apparently was extremely thirsty, so he said with longing, "Oh that one would give me drink of the water of the well of Bethlehem, which is by the gate!" In response, three of the mighty men, his most valiant and loyal warriors, broke through the camp of the Philistines, drew water from the well of Bethlehem, and brought it to David. Deeply moved he would not drink it, but poured it out as an offering to the Lord. "Be it far from me, O Lord, that I should [drink] this," he said. "Is not this the blood of the men that went in jeopardy of their lives?" (2 Sam. 23: 13-17; 1 Chron. 11:15-19)

DAVID'S LOYALTY: MEPHIBOSHETH

David's loyalty is well illustrated by his treatment of Mephibosheth, as recorded in 2 Samuel 9. Remembering his covenant with Jonathan, David inquired, "Is there yet any that is left of the house of Saul, that I may show him kindness for Jonathan's sake?" (v. 1). Ziba, a servant of Saul, was called before David. When questioned, he may have told the brief account found in 2 Samuel 4:4 of Jonathan's son Mephibosheth. Ziba said Mephibosheth lived in the home of Machir in the village of Lo-debar (v. 4).

David brought Mephibosheth to Jerusalem and was so moved when he met him, he restored him Saul's entire estate. David also said to him, "Thou shalt eat bread at my table continually" (v. 7). This meant that Mephibosheth was being adopted as a son by David. In addition, Ziba was commanded by David to till the land of the estate and bring the harvest to Mephibosheth.

Putting Truth into Action

1. What's a situation you're facing now in which a healthy fear of God might help you do the right thing?
2. What part of worship do you feel a need to know more about? How will you go about learning more?
3. When was a time you did the wrong thing for a good reason? How might you avoid making a similar mistake again?
4. Discuss ways that a husband and wife can keep from drifting apart.
5. How does David's description of the ideal city of God's house, as found in Psalm 15, apply in today's world?

CHAPTER 7

Great Promises from a Faithful God

2 Samuel 7 through 10
1 Chronicles 17 through 19

One of the great practical values of the Bible is the assurance and reassurance it gives us of the power of God and His faithfulness to His promises over the centuries. We see in its pages, for example, that much about Jesus' life, death, and resurrection was prophesied hundreds of years before, and we're comforted with the assurance that God will fulfill His promises to us as well.

In the next phase of David's life, we see not only more of the foreshadowings of Jesus the Messiah, but also how God will honor and bless a person whose heart is totally given to worshiping and serving Him. It's easy to get discouraged when we're in difficult circumstances, but David's example at this time shows that indeed, "Blessed is the man that walketh not in the counsel of the ungodly . . . But his delight is in the law of the Lord . . . and whatsoever he doeth shall prosper" (Psa. 1:1-3).

Now came a period when God gave David rest from all his enemies far and near. It was obvious to Nathan the prophet that David was the apple of God's eye (Psa. 17:8). So when the king suggested he would like to build a house, or temple, for Jehovah, Nathan replied, "Go, do all that is in thine heart; for the Lord is with thee" (2 Sam. 7:3). But that same night, God said to Nathan, "Go and tell David, my servant, Thus saith the Lord, Thou shalt not build me an house to dwell in" (1 Chron. 17:4).

The reproved Nathan explained to David that God had walked with Israel since He brought them out of Egypt and had never commanded a shepherd of Israel to build a "house of cedars." When God wanted a stationary house to be built, He would so state and would furnish the plans. The lessons to be learned from this incident are clear: (1) our wants aren't necessarily God's wants, and (2) we can't anticipate God. He would be a small God, indeed, if we could.

Nathan is a classic example of a sincere man's assuming some good project would be pleasing to God without first checking with God. We today can so easily bid God speed to some religious project that appears to be good without first being sure it conforms to God's will.

Much later, David added a postscript to what God had told him. He told his son Solomon, "It was in my mind to build an house unto the name of the Lord my God: But the word of the Lord came to me, saying, Thou has shed blood abundantly, and hast made great wars: thou shalt not build an house unto my name" (1 Chron. 22:7-8). But if David could not build God's temple, he could and did collect vast amounts of supplies to go into the building.

GOD'S GREAT PROMISE TO DAVID

God wasn't angry with David. In fact, in telling David not to build, He made him a great promise.

God said: "I took thee from the sheep cote . . . to be ruler over my people and I was with thee whithersoever thou wentest, and have cut off all thine enemies out of thy sight, and have made thee a great name. Also the Lord telleth thee that he will make thee an house." Then He said that when David died, He would place his seed on the throne, "and I will establish the throne of his kingdom for ever" (2 Sam. 7:8-13).

In 1 Chronicles 22, Solomon is singled out as the immediate son of David who was chosen to build a material temple to Jehovah. But the more distant fulfillment was in the seed of David, Jesus, who built the spiritual temple of God, the church, and overshadowed the more immediate fulfillment. Did David understand the immensity of God's promise? Indeed he did, because the Scriptures say of David, "Therefore being a prophet, and knowing that God had sworn with an oath to him, that of the fruit of his loins, according to the flesh, he would raise up Christ to sit on his throne" (Acts 2:20).[1]

Isaiah the prophet certainly understood that the Messiah was to come through David (Isa. 9:6-7). The prophet Jeremiah understood it, saying, "Behold, the days come, saith the Lord, that I will raise unto David a righteous Branch, and a King shall reign and prosper, and shall execute judgment and justice in the earth" (Jer. 23:5; see also 33:15-16). Most of all, Mary understood, because the announcing angel told her she would bring forth a son who was both the Son of God and the son of David (Luke 1:30-33).[2]

David responded to the gracious promises of Jehovah with humility: "Who am I, O Lord God . . . that thou hast brought me hitherto?" (2 Sam. 7:18). And in humility he accepted God's promise: "Thou O Lord God, hast spoken it: and with thy blessing let the house of thy servant be blessed for ever" (2 Sam. 7:29).

In connection with this high point in David's life, there are several psalms worth considering. Psalm 16 is a beautiful statement of God's place in David's life. He wrote, "The Lord is the portion of mine inheritance.... yea, I have a goodly heritage ... because he is at my right hand, I shall not be moved" (v. 5, 6, 8). For David, as it was with Paul, "to depart" was "to be with Christ" (Phil. 1:23); "For thou wilt not leave my soul in hell.... Thou wilt show me the path of life," David said (vv. 10-11).

It is a poor, mean view that speaks of a Christian's life as a preparation for death. It's a preparation for eternal life!

Psalm 2 is a short, messianic psalm often quoted in the New Testament. Verses 1 and 2 are quoted in Acts 4:25-26, and verse 7 is quoted in Acts 13:33, Hebrews 1:5, and Hebrews 5:5. The psalm reads in part, "The Lord hath said unto me, Thou art my Son; this day have I begotten thee.... Kiss the Son, lest he be angry, and ye perish from the way.... Blessed are all they that put their trust in him" (vv. 7, 12).

THE BREAKING CREST

Second Samuel 8-12 and 1 Chronicles 18-20 deal with a period of ten or more years in David's life during which the chronology of events is uncertain. Victories were won on many fronts, pushing the boundaries of David's kingdom ever wider. It was a period when "David executed judgment and justice unto all his people" (2 Sam. 8:15) and firmly established the Hebrew nation as a commanding influence in the region.

This period was also a time when David's life and career were at crest, but like every great wave on an ocean, the crest cannot be maintained or frozen. The crest will break amid much spume and roar, or it will lose its momentum and simply flatten into the sea around it. David's wave shattered on his adultery with Bathsheba and the murder of Uriah, her husband. This episode and the anticipation of it causes all the other events of this period to lose significance; therefore, this writer will, as did the inspired writers, summarize.

"In the course of time, the king of the Ammonites died, and his son, Hanun succeeded him as king. David thought, I will show kindness to Hanun, son of Nahash, just as his father showed kindness to me. So David sent a delegation to express his sympathy to Hanun concerning his father." (2 Sam. 10:1-2; see also 1 Chron. 19:1-2, NIV) But, when they arrived Hanun treated them as spies. He had their full beards, which were so cherished by the dignified Jews, shaved from one side of their faces. This would indicate that they were two-faced. As if this indignity were not enough, he had their robes cut off right in the middle of their buttocks, and thus, this dignified delegation from David was set free half naked and half shaven. Ammon was east of the Jordan River, so when the delegation got to Jericho, they sent runners to David to tell him of their treatment. He saw no humor in the treatment Hanun had given to his personal representatives, but he did show compassion to the delegation. He sent word for them to remain at Jericho until their beards grew out.

Hanun and the Ammonites, realizing that David and Israel would surely strike back, hired the Syrians with their 33,000 men to fight their battle for them. David sent his great general Joab, who against overwhelming odds, inspired his men before the battle with the short charge, "Courage! We must really act like men today if we are going to save our people and the cities of our God. God will do what is his good will" (See 2 Samuel 10:12). What a wonderful message! We today must also have the courage, against great odds, to let God use us. He will do what is His good will!

The battle began and presently the Syrians fell back to regroup. In a later battle they were defeated decisively. Thus, the sphere of David's empire and influence was pushed far to the north and west. Tribute money began to flow into Jerusalem, riches that later would make Solomon the richest king on earth.

David smote Moab (the reason is not given) and commanded that all the prisoners were to lie down on the ground. He then divided them into thirds by measuring with a length of cord. At a random pick one third of the Moabites were allowed to live and two thirds were slaughtered. David was as skilled at brutality as he was at praise. The remaining "Moabites became servants to David and brought tribute" (2 Sam. 8:2).

To the south David also placed garrisons throughout Edom and "all the Edomites became subject to David. The Lord gave David victory everywhere he went" (2 Sam. 8:14, NIV).

THE EMPIRE OF DAVID

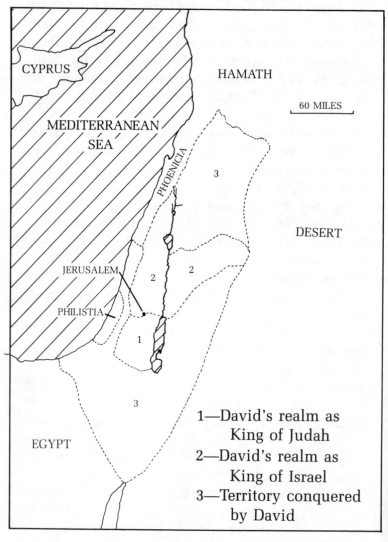

CYPRUS

HAMATH

60 MILES

MEDITERRANEAN
SEA

PHOENICIA

3

DESERT

JERUSALEM

2

2

PHILISTIA

1

3

EGYPT

1—David's realm as
   King of Judah
2—David's realm as
   King of Israel
3—Territory conquered
   by David

During this phase of David's life three psalms are typical of his relationship to God.

> "May the Lord answer you when you are in distress;
> . . . and grant you support from Zion.
> May he remember all your sacrifices
> . . . (and) give you the desire of your heart
> and make all your plans succeed."
>
> Ps. 20:1-4, NIV

Psalm 20 appears to have been composed when David was about to go into battle against a foreign enemy. It was written to be sung by the high priest and the people in the courtyard of the tabernacle David had raised in Jerusalem to house the Ark of God. It was a prayer petitioning God to be with the king and give him victory. If this request of the people for David their king sounds a little too broad for a mere man, we must remember that this psalm, as John Calvin pointed out, doubtless may be regarded as the prayer of Christians for their King, Jesus. Do we today pray zealously for the victory of Christ over all the forces of evil, or do we forget that Christ's spiritual kingdom is surrounded by enemies bent on its destruction, even as David's physical kingdom was surrounded by enemy nations? Jesus taught His disciples to pray daily, "Thy kingdom come" (Matt. 6:10). Certainly today His disciples should pray, "Thy kingdom prevail."[3]

After the victory comes the national thanksgiving, and so Psalm 21 is to Psalm 20. In Psalm 20 the people had requested God to give their king his heart's desire, and in Psalm 21:2 they happily sing, "Thou hast given him in his heart's desire." Far too often we forget to thank the Lord after He blesses us.

In a campaign against the forces of evil, there will be setbacks, and Psalm 60 shows us how David handled his. There's a sudden switch in mood that occurs between verses 3 and 6. This was David's typical approach to prayer. His faith in God's promises was so strong that all it took to trigger his "high" was a prayer. He was addicted to prayer! He knew that in prosperous days there were many sources of help, but in the hour of trouble there was but one. That source, God, was approached through prayer.

David Fights Another Giant

Recorded almost as an afterthought in 2 Samuel 21:15-17 is an incident that had an important bearing on David's later tragic sin. In one of the battles with the Philistines, David engaged in a personal duel with Ishbi-benob, a son of the giant. Ishbi-benob was a massive man whose bronze spearhead weighed close to seven and a half pounds. The scripture says, "And David ... became faint," and it appeared as if Ishbi-benob would slay David. But Joab's brother Abishai came to his rescue and killed the Philistine.[4]

David's becoming faint and having to be rescued meant one thing to his men: he was over the hill as an active battlefield soldier. For him to continue fighting would not only imperil his life and all he meant to Israel, but also the lives of the companions fighting next to him. This time the weak link was saved, but in a battle where the stakes were life and death, the weak link had to be removed. "Then the men of David sware unto him, saying, Thou shalt go no more out with us to battle, that thou quench not the light of Israel" (v. 17). David was nearing fifty, and he had led a long life as a soldier. But it doesn't matter how old a man is when the words "never more" are applied to him; they always fall like a sledgehammer. David knew that when one leaf falls, it won't be long before others follow and the cold winter of old age sets in.

Putting Truth into Action

1. Are any problems you have due to hastiness such as Nathan displayed?
2. David kept a promise to Jonathan by caring for Mephibosheth. What promise to God or another person do you need to give more attention to?
3. If life here should be preparing us for eternity, how might that perspective cause us to live differently?
4. David had a healthy "addiction" to prayer; it quickly restored his hope and faith in God. What's your typical reaction to prayer? Why?
5. How could David be so compassionate at times and so cruel at others? How do you account for the opposites in your life?

CHAPTER 8

Even the Best Can Fall

2 Samuel 11 and 12

Regarding temptation and sin, Martin Luther once said, "You can't keep the birds from flying over your head, but you can keep them from building a nest in your hair." Being tempted to sin is a part of being human, and none of us ever reaches a point of being immune to its appeal. In fact, the greatest trials seem to befall those who are closest to God, as Satan seeks to ruin their witness.

We've seen in David's words and actions a good part of why he was known as a man after God's own heart. In many ways he's a good model for us today, and as tragic as his sin with Bathsheba was, in a sense we shouldn't be surprised that it could happen. The fact it did should warn us to stay on guard against temptation every day.

DAVID AND BATHSHEBA

"In the spring, at the time when kings go off to war, David sent Joab out with the king's men ... and besieged Rabbah. But David remained in Jerusalem" (2 Sam. 11:1, NIV; see also 1 Chron. 20:1). The inspired scribe of Chronicles went directly from verse 1 to David's going down and taking the crown from the head of the defeated king of Rabbah. However, the inspired scribe of Samuel used fifty-one verses between verse 1 and the victory over Rabbah to tell of David's adulterous affair with Bathsheba. Perhaps God thought once was enough to tell of the shame of David.

As his army marched off to fight without him, David must have felt restless, lonely, and unneeded. There are times in everyone's life when such feelings cloud the mind so as to preclude clear thinking. The feeling that the world can go on about its business without you is depressing. Possibly in such a melancholy mood, David was pacing the flat roof of his palace when, in the soft light of the day's closing, he saw a beautiful woman bathing. His sexual nature was tempted to lust after her.

Instead of controlling his desires and turning away, which would have shown moral and spiritual strength, he made the effort to find out who she was. He knew that any woman he saw bathing was probably attached to the house of a loyal follower, because the houses of trusted associates, men of rank and power, were built around his own. But this did not deter him. He found out she was the wife of Uriah, one of his mighty men who had been loyal to him from the days in the cave of Adullam. She was also the granddaughter of Ahithophel, a seer and trusted counselor in David's court. None of this deterred him. He knew, too, that Uriah was away fighting with his army. So he sent for Bathsheba, and when she came, he had illicit sexual relations with her.

What kind of woman Bathsheba was and whether she complied with his wishes willingly or unwillingly has no bearing on David's guilt. The law that King David was committed to uphold read, "And the man that committeth adultery with another man's wife, even he that committeth adultery with his neighbor's wife, the adulterer and the adulteress shall surely be put to death" (Lev. 20:10).

David sent Bathsheba back to Uriah's house, probably thinking that was the end of the incident. But Uriah's wife conceived, and she sent word to David, "I am pregnant with your child." How long after the adulterous act did she send the message that brought fear to the mind of David? The Bible tells us Bathsheba had just completed the purification rites after menstruation when she and David committed adultery (2 Sam. 11:4). Therefore, she could have sent the note after a month, but most likely there was an interval of two months.

So David sent word to Joab, instructing him to send Uriah back to Jerusalem. When he arrived, David asked him how the war was going, then told him to go home and relax (2 Sam. 11:6-8). How smooth and suave David acted here, and how wicked! And the coverup should have worked. One thing is for certain, though: David could not, nor can we, cover up sin from an all-seeing God. David's coverup didn't work because Uriah did not go to his house and relax with his wife. He felt it wouldn't be right for him to enjoy the comforts of his home and wife while Joab and all his fellow soldiers were camping out. David was disappointed, needless to say, but he didn't give up. He had Uriah eat and drink with him and got Uriah drunk, thinking alcohol would loosen Uriah's convictions. However, when evening came, the old soldier went to bed not with his wife, but on his mat with the servants.

David, seeing his coverup had failed, then decided to have Uriah killed quickly so he might marry Bathsheba and claim the child as rightly being his. This cold-hearted plan came from the side of David that's strange to us. When a person who is capable of great goodness submits to the temptation of the Evil One, he becomes equally capable of great wickedness. David wrote a letter to Joab instructing him to put Uriah at the front of the hottest part of the battle and then pull back, leaving him there to die. David even had the gall to have Uriah deliver the sealed orders! (2 Sam. 11:14-15).

Joab followed his commander-in-chief's instructions, and Uriah was killed along with other soldiers of Israel in a reckless and militarily unnecessary maneuver. David was notified of Uriah's death, as was Bathsheba, and she mourned for him the established period of time. Afterward, King David and Bathsheba were married, "but the thing David had done displeased the Lord" (2 Sam. 11:27, NIV). "Oh, what a tangled web we weave, when first we practice to deceive," (wrote the poet Sir Walter Scott). Said the apostle James, "When lust hath conceived it bringeth forth sin: and sin, when it is finished, bringeth forth death" (James 1:15).

PSALMS OF THE PERIOD

In spite of David's great sins, the period surrounding those events was his most prolific psalm-writing time. The psalms were predominantly psalms of praise for and trust in God. They became more didactic as he defined his ideals, and the Messianic element was strong.

Psalm 110, for example, was used by Jesus to confront the Pharisees with His claim to be the Messiah. They acknowledged the Christ was to be a descendant of David. "He saith unto them, How then doth David in spirit call him Lord, saying, The Lord said unto my Lord, Sit thou on my right hand, till I make thine enemies thy footstool? If David then call him Lord, how is he his son?" (Matt. 22:43-45). This is one of five quotations of Psalm 110:1 in the New Testament, and it's referred to in three other places as well, making it the most frequently quoted verse from the Old Testament in the New.

The phrase "in the spirit" is used in the Bible to mean "under the influence of the Holy Spirit," and in verse 1 it was so used. "David in the spirit" was given a new and exciting revelation by Jehovah. The Messiah would not only be the King of kings in Zion, but He would also be the highest priest, a "priest for ever after the order of Melchizedek" (v. 4). This passage became the basis of the argument for the superiority of Jesus' priesthood as found in Hebrews 5-10.

Psalm 8 is another outstanding song from this period, one of the most beautiful of David's psalms of praise. Its opening and closing sentence is the majestic "O Lord our Lord, how excellent is thy name in all the earth!"

When we consider the majesty of God and the smallness of mankind, is it possible not to wonder why God bothers with us? David wondered this, too, and then answered our wondering: "When I consider thy heavens, the work of thy fingers, the moon and the stars, which thou hast ordained; what is man, that thou art mindful of him? ... For thou hast made him a little lower than the angels, and hast crowned him with glory and honor. Thou madest him to have dominion over the works of thy hands; thou hast put all things under his feet" (vv. 3-6).

Clearly, David was a man who really loved God and wanted to be like Him. At many times he was God's faithful image. But in some things he failed miserably.

David may have already found that the zest of life is discovered in the quest for a great goal rather than the attaining of it. He seemed to feel a loss of purpose, the let-down feeling that comes after the long-sought-after prize is won. This psychological phenomenon is observable in all fields of human endeavor.

Thus, there's all the more reason for us to set a place in heaven with our Lord as our goal. We can then stretch forward to the things ahead of us and "press on toward the goal" until we make our exit from this world (Phil. 3:13-14, NIV). Other goals in our lives should be only milestones in our great quest, because the best in this life is to be found in the striving, the suffering, the searching. And not just the best, but also the safest, for the hoping and uncertainty of the quest keep us alert to every danger.

The Harassed King

When Joab was ready to capture Rabbah, he sent a message to David that it was time for him to come with the rest of the army. If David did not move quickly, the city and its king would capitulate to Joab, and he would receive the credit for its capture, a credit Joab felt should go to David the king. So David came and took the city.

"And he [David] brought out the people that were in it, and cut them with saws, and with harrows of iron, and with axes" (1 Chron. 20:3), "and made them pass through the brickkiln" (2 Sam. 12:31). This King James Version has David acting barbarously, killing the inhabitants in most cruel and torturous manners. Some modern translations and paraphrases make an effort to interpret these passages in a more favorable manner for David, saying he put the inhabitants of Rabbah to work with saws, harrows, and axes and at the brick factory. Either interpretation may be accepted, but the weight of scholarship leans toward the former. This would mean that David was for the second time at apogee in his relationship with God. Sin with all of its power was pulling David away from goodness.

There should be no doubt that in the months following the death of Uriah and the taking of his wife, David's conscience bothered him. It undoubtedly caused him to be morose and mean. Verses 3-4 of Psalm 32 confirm this: "When I kept silent, my bones wasted away through my groaning all day long. For day and night your hand was heavy upon me: my strength was sapped as in the heat of summer" (NIV).

Nine months after the original sin, Bathsheba bore David a son. Maybe by then David's self-reproaches became less frequent and less agitating, but as Matthew Henry well observed, "His harp was out of tune, and his soul was like a tree in winter, with the life in the root only." This son had cost him greatly, and he loved him dearly.

What David had done had displeased the Lord, but the Lord had not judged. Was He waiting to see if David would confess and repent? One thing is certain; God had not slumbered, nor was He indifferent to David's sin, but He was in no haste. God seeks the right time (the fullness of time) and is not concerned, as we are, with whether it is arrived at quickly or slowly. "But do not forget this one thing, dear friends: With the Lord a day is like a thousand years, and a thousand years are like a day. The Lord is not slow in keeping his promise, as some understand slowness. He is patient with you, not wanting anyone to perish, but everyone to come to repentance. But the day of the Lord will come like a thief" (2 Pet. 3:8-10, NIV).

NATHAN REBUKES DAVID

"The day of the Lord" came at last for David. God sent His prophet Nathan to David with a parable and a judgment. Nathan must be given credit for being a courageous proclaimer of God's word, for a person did not go before a king without risking his life, especially to condemn the king. But it was part of the duty of God's prophet.

The parable Nathan used to convict David was a masterpiece. It appealed to David's basic senses of justice and compassion. Two men were dwelling in a city. One was rich, possessing flocks and herds innumerable. The other was poor, having only one lamb, which he brought up in his house and loved as he would a daughter. Then a traveler came to visit the rich man, and having to entertain the traveler, the rich man took the poor man's one lamb and roasted and served it instead of killing a lamb from his many flocks.[1]

At this point in the parable, David didn't wish to hear any more. His anger was hot against the evil rich man, "and he said to Nathan, As the Lord liveth, the man that hath done this thing shall surely die: and he shall restore the lamb fourfold . . . because he had no pity" (2 Sam. 12:5-6). David's judgment was lawful according to Exodus 22:1, and that would have been "case closed" if left to David.

But suddenly the prophet said explosively, "Thou art the man!" David had condemned himself, and before he could react in self-defense, the prophet continued. The Lord made you king and delivered you from Saul, Nathan said, and if that hadn't been enough, He would have given you more. "Wherefore hast thou despised the commandment of the Lord, to do evil in his sight?" (2 Sam. 12:9).[2] Nathan painted an evil portrait of an ungrateful David, interested only in satisfying his own lusts.

The Bible doesn't indicate whether Nathan paused for a response after stating God's charge against David, or whether he immediately continued by stating the punishment that would come upon David. David may well have been in a state of shock, because he was seeing himself as he had become, perhaps for the first time.

God's punishment was threefold: (1) The sword (serious troubles) would never depart from David's house. God would raise up evil against him out of his own family. (2) God would take his wives before his eyes and give them to his neighbor, who would sleep with them. God said, "You did it in secret, but I will do this thing in broad daylight before all

Israel" (2 Sam. 12:12). (3) His son by Bathsheba would die.[3]

Before Nathan could complete the judgment of God upon David, David cried out, "I have sinned against the Lord" (2 Sam. 12:13). He made no effort at rationalizing. There were no excuses, just a complete confession of sin. That this confession was sincere and the result of heartfelt repentance is manifested by the seven psalms connected to this confession and, most of all, by God's accepting it as sincere. Our God is so eager and so quick to forgive! Nathan told David, "The Lord also hath put away thy sin; thou shalt not die" (2 Sam. 12:13).

Before leaving, Nathan helped David understand the unmerited grace of God. In substance he said, "The Lord has forgiven you even though you, through your sins, have given the enemies of God great reason to blaspheme. God's pure and holy name is being dragged through the mire of shame because you, His servant, have acted so wickedly. Your sins are such as require death. You will not die, but to satisfy the law, the son born to you of Bathsheba will die."

PSALMS OF REPENTANCE

When Nathan left David's court, David was alone with his thoughts. This was when he wrote: "I am weary with my groaning; all the night I make my bed to swim; I water my couch with my tears. Mine eye is consumed because of grief" (Psa. 6:6-7). It was also then that he pleaded with the Lord: "O Lord, rebuke me not in thine anger, neither chasten me in thy hot displeasure. Have mercy upon me. O

Lord; for I am weak: O Lord, heal me; for my bones are vexed" (Psa. 6:1-2).

In the closing lines of the short sixth Psalm, the deep penitence of the real David, the David of absolute faith in God's love, clearly apperars.

It is so easy to pray when one is in trouble. Often when all is well with us, our prayers may be vague like an arrow shot heavenward with a slack string, but when we are in trouble, our prayers are like an arrow shot from a full-bent bow, straight at the mark.

The heading of Psalm 51 places it after the visit of Nathan. David began with a plea for mercy and confession: "Have mercy upon me, O God, according to thy loving-kindness: according unto the multitude of thy tender mercies blot out my transgressions. Wash me thoroughly from mine iniquity, and cleanse me from my sin. For I acknowledge transgressions: and my sin is ever before me. . . . Purge me with hyssop, and I shall be clean: wash me, and I shall be whiter than snow" (Psa. 51:1-3, 7).

Note the synonyms for sin used by David to describe his actions—"transgressions" and "iniquity"— and the terms describing the results of God's forgiveness—"blot out," "cleanse," "purify," and "wash." It was the putting off of the old man in symbolic death and the beginning of a new life in rebirth. "Create in me a clean heart, O God; and renew a right spirit within me" (v. 10). David's description of his rededication was strikingly similar to the doctrine of salvation as taught in the New Testament (see, e.g., John 3:3-5; Rom. 6:4).

David remembered that God had taken His Holy Spirit from Saul when he sinned. Thus he pleaded, "Cast me not away from thy presence; and take not thy Holy Spirit from me" (v. 11).

David acknowledged in verses 15-17 that God was not nearly as pleased with burnt offerings as He was with the sacrifice of "a broken and a contrite heart." This was what David offered to God. It has been said that "this psalm is like a page of an autobiography written in the author's lifeblood" *(The Pulpit Commentary).*[4]

Of the seven penitential psalms found in the book of Psalms, the third and final one that seems connected to David's great sin is Psalm 32. Verses 1-2 were quoted by the apostle Paul in Romans 4:6-8 in his argument on the importance of faith. When God does not impute sin to an individual's soul, it isn't that He's playing favorites, but because He knows the true condition of the inner person. As David stated in verse 10, "Many sorrows shall be to the wicked: but he that trusteth in the Lord, mercy shall compass him about." Those who are without guile in their spiritual lives (v. 2) are wrapped in God's love and forgiveness.

In verse 6, David taught a lesson much needed in every generation: "Let everyone who is godly pray to you while you may be found; surely when the mighty waters rise, they will not reach him" (NIV).

THE SON DIES

In fulfillment of God's judgment against David, the son of David and Bathsheba became very ill, and for a whole week, while the innocent child struggled to live, David prayed. He fasted and lay on the ground. What indescribable grief David brought upon himself when the consequences of his sin began to unfold! The Bible scholar Hale has observed that starting with the visit from Nathan, "the remainder of David's life was as disastrous as the beginning had been prosperous." Indeed, the subsequent suffering of David would be inexplicable if his great transgression had not been recorded.[5]

Herein lies one of the internal proofs of the inspiration of the Bible: the Bible reveals the evil deeds of its greatest heroes as well as their many righteous deeds, showing there is but one worthy of being called reverend (Psa. 111:9) and thus worthy of worship (Matt. 4:10).

The child died, and after David heard of it, his servants were amazed to see him get up from the ground, bathe, and dress in fresh clothes. He went first to the tabernacle and worshipped, then went home and ate. He explained his actions in these words: "While the child was yet alive, I fasted and wept: for I said, Who can tell whether God will be gracious to me, that the child may live? But now he is dead, wherefore should I fast? can I bring him back again? I shall go to him, but he shall not return to me?" (2 Sam. 12:22-23). This was a noble statement of deference to the will of God. True religion is submission to God's will even when we cannot understand why—a willingness to say, "Thy will be done. Praise be to God, for He is holy."

SOLOMON IS BORN

David, feeling his responsibility, comforted Bathsheba, and in due time she bore a second son who was favored by Jehovah. Nathan was sent by the Lord to call the child Jedidiah, which means "Beloved of God." David knew that God had earlier promised him a son who would be a man of peace, and that his name would be Solomon (peaceful). (1 Chron. 22:9). Therefore, David called the child Solomon and promised Bathsheba he would be the next king. (1 Kings 1:30). Later it will seem David forgot this promise until he was reminded of it. Promises are so frequently forgotten by men, but God is not negligent concerning His promises (2 Pet. 3:9).

At the time Solomon was born, his father was approximately fifty-two; his oldest half-brother, Amnon, was around nineteen; Absalom, another half-brother, was around eighteen; and his only half-sister, the full sister of Absalom, Tamar, was seventeen years of age. The following chart of David's wives and children may be helpful as we enter the period of David's life when his children's activities controlled his own.

David's Wives and Children

WIVES (8)	SONS (17)	DAUGHTERS (1)
Michal Saul's daughter		

Abigail
  Nabal's wife
	Chileab, or Daniel
	  (2nd born)	

Ahinoam	Amnon (1st born)	

Maacah
  Daughter of Talmai,
  king of Geshur
	Absalom (3rd born)	Tamar

Haggith	Adonijah (4th born)	
Abital	Shephatiah (5th born)	
Eglah	Ithream (6th born)	
Bathsheba Uriah's wife	Solomon (7th born) Shimea Nathan Shobab	
	(mothers and birth order unassigned) Ibhar Elishua Nepheg Japhia Eliada Elishama, or Beeliada Eliphelet	

The years following the return of David to God's grace were busy. David's kingdom far exceeded in size the land promised by God to the descendants of Abraham. Its eastern border skirted the edge of the great desert and extended southward to where Arabah touched an arm of the Red Sea at Ezion-geber. Northwestward from there, the border ran all the way to the river Nile of Egypt. The coast of the great Mediterranean Sea formed the western boundary, and northward it ran to the land of the Phoenicians with whom David had friendly relations through King Hiram of Troy. Inland, the northern border extended into the desert north of Damascus, Syria.

As David gained victories on the battlefield, he also collected great supplies of gold, silver, brass, and iron. These he dedicated to Jehovah for the building of the future temple. David later told Solomon he had collected 1.4 million pounds of gold, 14 million pounds of silver, brass and iron beyond weighing, as well as timber and stone (1 Chron. 22:14).

David's nature was like a spring of water in the mountains that, though choked and buried beneath a heap of rocks and rubbish, yet finds its way again to the surface. The simple purity and devotion of David's character, though sometimes polluted by lust and sin, always rose again in trust and faith.

Putting Truth into Action

1. Describe the series of sins that began with David's lusting after Bathsheba. Why does one sin tend to lead to another?

2. At what times in life are we most vulnerable to temptation? Knowing that, what special precautions can we take at such times?

3. Besides restoring our relationship with God, how does confession of sin help us?

4. Discuss Psalm 32, particularly verse 2.

CHAPTER 9

Crushed by Consequences

2 Samuel 13, 14 and 21
1 Chronicles 21 and 22

I remember learning in a high school physics class that for every physical action, there's an equal and opposite reaction. I also learned, at a much earlier age in my mother's kitchen, that when you heat water to 212 degrees Fahrenheit, it begins to boil and steam away. My point is simply that there are physical laws governing our world, and once we set things in motion, those laws take over regardless of our intentions.

After David confessed his sins related to Bathsheba, he had a clean slate with God, just as we do when we confess our sins (1 John 1:9). But sin, like physical actions, has consequences, and once sin is committed, its consequences are usually felt for some time thereafter. The fact that David had confessed did not overturn the effects of his sins on himself and his family.

As we look in this chapter at a difficult period in David's life, may it impress upon us the long-term consequences of our own choices. And let's not jump to judge David harshly but rather bear in mind that if David were prone to such sin and poor judgment, how much more so are we. "Wherefore let him that thinketh he standeth take heed lest he fall" (1 Cor. 10:12).

THE CALDRON BOILS

While outwardly David prospered after the incident with Bathsheba, inwardly his family was boiling with lust and intrigue that would break forth to shake his empire and bring the punishment God had decreed.

David's sons had the wealth of this world that he had not enjoyed as a boy, but they did not have in their polygamous environment the inner wealth from discipline and training that David had received. David spoiled his sons, which is evidenced both by their selfish behavior and by the statement found in 1 Kings 1:6: "His [Adonijah's] father had never interfered with him by asking, 'Why do you behave as you do?' " (NIV).

Amnon, David's oldest son, was an example of the person produced by such an undisciplined environment. Instead of training to be a strong and industrious leader, he moped about like a lovesick calf because he lusted after his younger half-sister Tamar. Tamar was around sixteen and lovely. She was the virgin daughter of Maacah and the sister of Absalom, who was as handsome as his younger sister was fair.

Jonadab, a cousin to Amnon, known for his craftiness, observed how haggard Amnon looked and inquired concerning his health. Amnon confessed his love for Tamar. With so many loyal sons and close cousins, the intrigue must have been lively. And Jonadab, to gain "points" with Amnon, the first in line for the throne, suggested Amnon pretend he was sick and ask his father to send Tamar to care for him (2 Sam. 13:5).

Amnon deceived his father as Jonadab had suggested, and David sent a message to Tamar to go and prepare food for her half-brother. She obediently went to serve him, and he sent out all his servants and had her bring the food into his bedchamber so she might hand-feed him. When she did as he bade, he took hold of her and raped her. She begged him not to commit such folly for both her sake and his, but he wouldn't listen. When he was done with her, he "hated her exceedingly; so that the hatred wherewith he hated her was greater than the love wherewith he had loved her" (2 Sam. 13:15). Then he had his servants throw her out and lock the door behind her.

Tamar made no attempt to cover up the incident. Rather, she placed ashes of mourning on her head, tore the colorful robe that virgin daughters of the king wore, and went to her quarters crying out loud so that attention was drawn to her.

ABSALOM'S REVENGE

David's reaction was one of great anger and undoubtedly of deep, inward pain, for Amnon's sin was a replay of his own. Children are often more prone to imitate their parents' vices than their virtues. If David as much as reproached Amnon orally, however, it is not recorded in the Bible. Both the Greek Septuagint and the Latin Vulgate add, "But he vexed not the spirit of Amnon, his son, because he loved him, because he was his first-born." Clearly, David had failed as a father, because the Bible teaches that if we love our children, we will discipline them (Heb. 12:5-11).

Absalom's response was typical of young men. His compassionate concern was quickly followed by the advice to Tamar, "Don't take it so seriously," while all the time he was inwardly burning with hatred and a desire for revenge. He had nothing to do with Amnon while he waited for their father to discipline him. When David did nothing, however, Absalom realized it would be up to him to avenge his sister. After all, was it not Simeon and Levi who killed Shechem when he had raped their sister Dinah? (Gen. 34).

Absalom nursed his wrath for two full years, thus lulling to sleep any suspicion on David's or Amnon's part that he might be harboring a spirit of revenge. Then an opportunity arose. Absalom had a flock of sheep at Baal-Hazor, which was about eight miles north of Jerusalem. The time of the shearing was at hand, which was always a time of feasting and celebration. Absalom invited all his brothers to share in his celebration, and went before his father to invite him to come and share in the occasion. David was probably pleased at both the industry and the thoughtfulness of his son Absalom, but not wishing to be a burden, he excused himself. The court of David by this time must have been so large that moving it even a few miles and entertaining it would have been an expensive matter.

When his father declined his invitation, Absalom insisted that his elder brother, Amnon, attend. David hesitated in giving permission but succumbed to Absalom's charms, blessing him in his endeavor and sending him on his way. Then Absalom commanded his servants to kill Amnon once they got him drunk (2 Sam. 13:28).[1]

When did this plot come into Absalom's mind? Was it only after his father had declined to attend the sheep-shearing, had he planned to have Amnon killed in their father's presence, or had he planned to have both his father and Amnon killed and take the throne for himself? We don't know, but we do know from the Scriptures that Absalom was ambitious, patient, deliberate, charming, and bold. I would guess he had been planning his course of action since at least the sheep-shearing of the prior year.

Absalom's servants killed Amnon as planned, and the other princes fled on their mules in panic.[2] Bad news travels fast, and bad news that's false travels even faster—faster than princes riding on mules. The first news that got to David was that "Absalom hath slain all the king's sons, and there is not one of them left" (2 Sam. 13:30). When David heard the report, he tore his robes and fell to the ground in complete misery. There blazed before his mind's eye the promise of the Lord that the sword would never depart from his house.

Though forgiven of the guilt by the Lord, did David ever release himself from the guilt? He had killed his faithful servant Uriah, and now his sons killed each other and raped their sisters. Would they have committed such grievous sins if he had not set the example before them?

Then Jonadab, the crafty nephew, broke into David's self-accusations and told him only Amnon was dead. Being a keen observer of human nature, Jonadab had seen the malice in Absalom's eyes and the tightness of his lips whenever he was around Amnon. How certain he was to make such a statement to the king!

But even as Jonadab was speaking, David's other sons were running into the palace area.

However, one of David's sons fled in a different direction—Absalom. Three times the Scriptures report, "Absalom fled." He was not only the son of a king, but also the grandson of a king. His mother was Maacah, daughter of Talmai, king of Geshur, and to Geshur Absalom fled. The location and size of Geshur are not known, but certainly David could have extradited Absalom if he had really wished to do so. However, Absalom had endeared himself to his father with his charisma. While David grieved mightily for Amnon, yet in his heart he knew Absalom had done what he would have done if he had been the brother of Tamar.

ABSALOM'S RETURN TO DAVID'S COURT

It had been nearly three years since Absalom had fled to his maternal grandfather's palace, and Joab could see how deeply David missed his son. He may have thought the people missed and sided with Absalom, too. But there was a stubborn streak in David that had to be broken before Absalom could come home. To break this barrier preventing a reconciliation, Joab "sent to Tekoah, and fetched thence a wise woman" (2 Sam. 14:2). Tekoah was a village only five miles south of Bethlehem.

From the biblical narrative, one might get the impression that the woman's acting skill surpassed her wisdom, because Joab told her what to do and how to appear. She put on mourner's apparel and acted like one who had long mourned for the dead. When she appeared before King David, she fell on her face, did obeisance, and cried out, "Help, O king" (2 Sam. 14:4). David asked what she wanted, and she told her fictional story. She claimed to be a widow and said one of her sons had killed the other, and now the rest of the family demanded that the surviving son be executed for murder. If that happened, she said, she would be left alone, and her husband's name would disappear because he had no surviving sons (2 Sam. 14:5-7).[3]

David was once again approached from his blind side by a parable that could hardly draw but one response from him. In the woman's story, justice was the villain, and forgiveness of the killer, who showed no remorse, was called for because of compassion for the widow. David ruled, "As the Lord liveth, there shall not one hair of thy son fall to the earth" (2 Sam. 14:11).

He undoubtedly thought that ruling would close the case, but the woman requested permission to continue. When permission was granted, she drew the application of her parable. Without calling Absalom by name, she left no doubt that David was the guilty one by not calling the banished son home. He was depriving the people of God of the heir apparent. Even as she portrayed Israel as the weeping mother, David was cast as the stern clansfolk who would deprive the mother of a second, though guilty, son.

The woman claimed to be expressing the feeling of the people of Israel, and maybe she was, because Absalom was much loved. It may be, on the other hand, that Joab chose to persuade David to recall Absalom not because of any personal affection, but to avert an insurrection that would have torn the kingdom apart.

The wise woman made two arguments to David that merit our notice. The first deals with the transitory nature of human life. She said, "For we must [all] needs die, and are as water spilt on the ground, which cannot be gathered up again" (2 Sam. 14:14). Since sin entered the world, death was and is inevitable. "It is appointed unto men once to die" (Heb. 9:27). Not only is death certain, but it's also final so far as this life is concerned.

This led to her second argument, namely, the great value God places on life. She declared that God, rather than taking away yet another life, "doth devise means, that his banished be not expelled from him" (2 Sam. 14:14). The best guess is that she was referring to the cities of refuge God provided under the law of Moses, but she was also foreshadowing the gospel of God's grace.[4]

David got the woman's message, but he also saw the hand of Joab in it. "Hide not from me . . . the thing that I shall ask thee," demanded David of the woman. "Is not the hand of Joab with thee in all this?" The wise woman quickly admitted to Joab's part in the matter and defended him as wanting to place the affair before his king in a new light. She was undoubtedly surprised that David could sense the source of her story. She paid David a compliment that any ruler would like to believe is true: "My lord has wisdom like that of an angel of God—he knows everything that happens in the land" (2 Sam. 14:20, NIV). A chief administrator who is not knowledgeable of the crosscurrents in his realm will not long remain as chief.

After dismissing the woman, David ordered Joab to bring Absalom back to Jerusalem. "Let him turn to his own house, and let him not see my face,"

David said (2 Sam. 14:24). He had granted Absalom's return, but had not granted him reconciliation or pardon. Now Absalom was back in Jerusalem, but not back in his father's favor.

Absalom's beauty was extraordinary. He was described as being without blemish from the soles of his feet to the crown of his head. His hair was his crowning glory, which he had cut only once a year, and then only because it weighed more than six pounds (2 Sam. 14:26). Such beauty is apt to excite vanity and pride in the one who possesses it, and vanity and pride are the roots of many sins. Augustine said, "Beauty is, indeed, a good gift of God; but that the good may not think it a great good, God dispenses it even to the wicked."

After living restricted to his house for two years, Absalom sent for Joab, but Joab would not come. So Absalom sent for him a second time, again in vain. Then Absalom had his servants set Joab's field of barley on fire, which got his attention! When Joab came to Absalom, Absalom sent him to his father with this message: "Wherefore am I come from Geshur? it had been good for me to have been there still: now therefore let me see the king's face; and if there be any iniquity in me, let him kill me" (2 Sam. 14:32). After Joab delivered the message, David called his son into his presence and was reconciled to him.

Absalom was finally pardoned and free to do as he wished, and he wished to be king. He began both to undermine his father and to win the confidence of the people for himself. He was a Machiavellian demagogue long before Prince Machiavellie was born. He had charisma and used it to steal away the hearts of the men of Israel (2 Sam. 15:6). While Absalom was in the process of readying himself for a coup against his father, other matters were claiming the attention and energy of David.

Two major calamities swept across David's kingdom. The first, a massive pestilence causing the death of 70,000 men, was brought on by David's decision to conduct a census of Israel. The second, a great famine, was God's retribution for something Saul had done prior to David's reign. There are scriptural uncertainties connected with both calamities, but it's still helpful to consider them.

David Takes a Census

The events leading to the deadly plague started when David decided to count the number of men of military age in his kingdom. He made the decision without consulting God and against the strong counsel of Joab (1 Chron. 21:3-4). Why did David decide to number the people? Because he responded positively to temptation from the Devil. First Chronicles 21:1 says, "And Satan stood up against Israel, and provoked David to number Israel." However, the account in 2 Samuel says God was angry at Israel and He moved David to number the people (2 Sam. 24:1). Who tempted David to sin? The Devil did, but with God's permission. We must remember that Satan cannot tempt a child of God without God's permission, but also that God's permission for a person to be tempted does not carry approval for the person tempted to do evil. Why God's anger was kindled against Israel, why David's taking a census at that time was a sin, and how the Devil tempted David we're not told.

David, not feeling threatened by any foreign power, assigned Joab and his captains the job of executing the census. It took them nine months and twenty days (2 Sam. 24:8). They started at the outskirts of Israel and proceeded inward toward Jerusalem. The count as given in 2 Samuel 24:9 was 800,000 men in Israel, 500,000 in Judah making a total of 1,300,000 men who drew the sword. If children, women, and old people had been counted, the kingdom would have had around 6,000,000 individuals. Compare that number to around 3,000,000 whom God had delivered from bondage in Egypt. However, there are problems with the count. In 1 Chronicles 21:5 the number for all Israel is given at 1,100,000 or 200,000 less than the number given in Samuel. Also, in the Chronicles record, Judah had 400,000 instead of the 500,000 recorded in Samuel.

In addition, it appears that David counted at least some of the Gentiles living within the boundaries of his kingdom because Joab and the counters "came to the stronghold of Tyre, and to all the cities of the Hivites, and of the Canaanites; and they went out to the south of Judah, even to Beersheba" (2 Sam. 24:7). Second Chronicles 2:17 reads, "Solomon took a census of all the aliens who were in Israel, after the census his father David had taken; and they were found to be 153,600" (NIV).

A third complication is found in 1 Chronicles 21:6 which reads, "But Levi and Benjamin counted he not among them: for the king's word was abominable to Joab." Thus, the census was not complete. The census numbers were so fouled up that they were not placed in the official records of King David because of God's wrath (1 Chron. 27:24). The authors of Samuel and Chronicles did not have official numbers to report; therefore, it is pointless to attempt to harmonize the figures found in the two accounts.

When David realized he had sinned by calling for a census and had begged God's forgiveness, God answered through Gad, David's seer. Gad explained that severe punishment was to befall Israel, and that David would have to choose from among three options: (1) he could choose three years of famine over the land, with all its misery; (2) he could choose three months of fleeing from enemies, which would entail a disastrous war; or (3) he could choose three days of plague in Israel, with all the deaths, terror, and sorrow that would bring. What a heart-squeezing, mind-paralyzing position David found himself in! War, plague, or famine? Three days, three months, or three years?

David certainly didn't wish to flee before his enemies. He had fled enough in his early life, and he had pursued enough as a general and king, to know that the mercies of God are much greater than the mercies of man. Therefore he replied, "Let us fall now into the hand of the Lord; for his mercies are great: and let me not fall into the hand of man" (2 Sam. 24:14).

A Plague on Israel

The Lord then sent a plague on Israel, and "there fell of Israel seventy thousand men" (1 Chron. 21:14). David had been right, however: the compassionate mercy of God had brought the plague to an early end (1 Chron. 21:15). But even so, what a price to pay for a foolish action! The deaths of 70,000 men, the grief in thousands of families, and the hardship brought on thousands of widows and orphans were all on David's conscience. How could he ever draw a happy breath again? We know he realized it was his responsibility, because when he saw the angel who was striking the people, he said to the Lord, "I have sinned, and I have done wickedly: but these sheep, what have they done? Let thine hand . . . be against me, and against my father's house" (2 Sam. 24:17).

The destroying angel halted at the outskirts of Jerusalem as it was then laid out. He stopped with sword drawn above the threshing floor of Araunah, the Jebusite, which was on Mount Moriah. (Araunah is called by a Hebrew variant "Ornan" at times.) The angel spoke to David through Gad and commanded him to set up an altar on the threshing floor of Araunah.

So David went to Araunah and asked to buy the site. Aranuah graciously offered everything—the threshing floor, the oxen, the wheat, and the wooden sledges—to David as a gift, but David refused to accept. Instead he enunciated a great principle: "I insist on paying the full price. I will not take for the Lord what is yours, or sacrifice a burnt offering that costs me nothing" (1 Chron. 21:24, NIV). A religion that does not cost one anything is worthless. Personal sacrifice is the sweet perfume that pleases the nostrils of God.

David bought the site and built an altar to the Lord there. When he had offered sacrifices and called upon the Lord, God sent fire from heaven upon the altar, even as He did when Moses had built the altar of the tabernacle in the wilderness (Lev. 9:24). Then the angel sheathed his sword at God's command, and David knew the God of Israel had answered him, ended the plague, and selected the site upon which the temple to His name should be built. This threshing floor was an appropriate site for God's house, because such floors were constructed, whenever possible, on an elevated outcropping of solid rock, where the wind could easily blow the chaff away. Solomon later built the temple of the Lord on that site.

Psalm 30 is a song of thanksgiving written after David was delivered from a great danger, possibly that of the plague looming over Jerusalem. The heading of the psalm says, "A song at the dedication of the house." A dedication usually comes after a house is completed, but David was elated that God had selected the side for His house and had allowed him to build an altar there. It is possible the dedication was for the altar as a representation of the completed temple. Jews today sing this psalm at their observance of the Feast of Dedication.

Two verses are special. Verse 5 says, "For his anger endureth but a moment: in his favor is life: weeping may endure for a night, but joy cometh in the morning." The length of God's anger depends on the quickness and sincerity of one's repentance. Verse 10 is a short prayer typical of David: "Hear, O Lord, and have mercy upon me: Lord, be thou my helper." We so often ask for God's help, but how often do we ask with the sense of "I'll do the work, Lord, if You will be my helper?"

Most psalms in the fourth book, or collection, of psalms do not have headings or authors ascribed to them, and Psalm 91 is among these. But if David didn't write it, it nonetheless fits the occasion well. In verses 3 and 6, it speaks of deliverance from the pestilence and of "the pestilence that walketh in darkness." The theme of this psalm is the security of the person who puts his trust in Jehovah: "A thousand shall fall at thy side, and ten thousand at thy right hand; but it shall not come nigh thee" (v. 7).

This psalm contains the promise from God that the Devil quoted as he tempted Christ in Luke 4: "For he shall give his angels charge over thee, to keep thee in all thy ways. They shall bear thee up in their hands, lest thou dash thy foot against a stone" (Psa. 91:11-12). We should find great comfort in the knowledge that angels are charged with our welfare if we fully place ourselves under the protective wings of God (Psa. 91:4).

A THREE-YEAR FAMINE

We see another example of the consequences of sin in 2 Samuel 21, where we're told of a three-year famine "in the days of David." We don't know the specific time in David's life that the famine occurred, but he felt the stress and sought a solution from the mouth of God. The Lord pronounced the guilt to be upon Saul and his family because he put the Gibeonites to death. In other words, Saul was the one who had sinned, but David, his successor, had to make atonement. There's an account in Joshua 9 of how the Gibeonites had outsmarted the Israelites and induced them to make a treaty some 500 years before David. Under that treaty, the Gibeonites had dwelt in peace with Israel as their servants down through the ages. But Saul, "in his zeal to the children of Israel and Judah," had slaughtered many of them.

David, learning the cause of the famine, went to the Gibeonites and asked what he could do to make atonement (2 Sam. 21:3). After making it clear they weren't interested in financial reparation, they said they wanted seven male descendants of Saul to be given to them to be hanged "unto the Lord in Gibeah of Saul" (vv. 4-6). David replied, "I will give them."

This may sound barbaric, but it was a small price for the genocidal action of Saul. Still, why did the time of judgment come in David's day rather than in Saul's? Why was a famine brought upon all the nation? We can only speculate.

When Saul was committing the evil, it was probably approved by the people of Israel. They undoubtedly profited from the property and land of the disposed Gibeonites. And when David came to power, he apparently did nothing to try to right the wrongs of his predecessor. Does God still hold us responsible for righting the wrongs committed by our predecessors?

God's actions are often not explained, nor do they have to be, because He is far more superior to the wisest of us than parents are to little children, and certainly wise parents do not attempt to justify all of their decisions to children because they are incapable of understanding the parent's reasoning. God said, "My thoughts are not your thoughts, neither are your ways my ways, saith the Lord. For as the heavens are higher than the earth, so are my ways higher than your ways, and my thoughts than your thoughts" (Isa. 55:8-9). Moses wrote, "The secret things belong unto the Lord our God: but those things which are revealed belong unto us and to our children for ever, that we may do all the words of this law" (Deut. 29:29). Moses stated a principle we desperately need to remember when things happen that we can't understand. Paul said in 2 Corinthians 5:7 that "we walk by faith, not by sight," or understanding, and we cannot walk by faith unless we fully accept the truth of the two verses quoted above.

As David began to choose the seven to hand over to the Gibeonites he spared Jonathan's son Mephibosheth. He took two of Saul's sons by Rizpah, a concubine, and five of Saul's grandsons by his oldest daughter Merab and her husband Adril (see 1 Sam. 18:19). The use of Michal's name as the mother of the five in 2 Samuel 21:8 is either a copyist's error or as Jamieson, Fausset, and Brown suggest in their commentary, Merab had died and Michal, her younger sister, had adopted them, for Michal was barren.

The seven descendants of Saul were sacrificed by the Gibeonites in April at the beginning of the barley harvest and the corpses remained exposed to the elements and to shame until the rains came, breaking the drought and indicating that God's wrath had been appeased. If the rains came at their usual time, it was six months later in October. For however long the corpses remained exposed, Rizpah, the mother of two of the victims, performed an act of devotion that touches the heart. She "took sackcloth and spread it out for herself on a rock. From the beginning of harvest till the rain poured down from the heaven on the bodies, she did not let the birds of the air touch them by day or the wild animals by night" (2 Sam. 21:10, NIV). When David heard of Rizpah's dedication, he sent and gathered the remains of the seven and buried them properly in the tomb of Kish, Saul's father, in the territory of

Benjamin. At this same time David had the remains of Saul and Jonathan returned and given proper burial.

Putting Truth into Action

1. What bad habits or practices of your parents, if any, have you tended to imitate? How have you begun to overcome them?

2. Since David did nothing to punish Amnon for raping Tamar, do you think Absalom was at all right to seek vengeance against Amnon? Why or why not? Are we ever justified in taking the law in our own hands? Why or why not?

3. Has God ever allowed anything in your life that you have a hard time understanding? How did you respond? What have you learned in this chapter that can help you deal with it?

4. Discuss the Devil's power to tempt us today.

5. If God were to hold us responsible for the actions of our forefathers to whom might you owe compensation?

CHAPTER 10

A Faith Greater Than Treachery

2 Samuel 15 and 16

The history of the world is filled with traitors. In our own country, a number of spies have been convicted in recent years of selling military secrets to the Soviet Union. Perhaps the most famous traitor in national history was Benedict Arnold, who helped the British during the American Revolution and whose name has become synonymous with treachery.

As David continued to suffer the consequences of his sin with Bathsheba, he fell victim to the treachery of a son and a man who had been a key adviser—two of the people closest to him. He was forced to run for his life once more.

In David's experiences at this time, we see further foreshadowing of the sufferings of Christ. We also see clearly the faith in God that sustained him through these fresh trials. Few of us have had armies chasing us with murder on their minds; and if God's grace were adequate for such adversity, which it was, we will find it more than adequate for our trials as well.

ABSALOM'S COUP

While David's days as king were filled with stressful matters, Absalom's days were filled with intrigue. He promoted himself by obtaining a chariot, horses (no mule for him), and fifty men to run before him and direct everyone's attention to him. He would get up early and greet people coming into Jerusalem from the provinces. When anyone would approach to bow down before him, he would reach out, take hold of him, and kiss him in the manner of that day. To anyone who had a judicial claim of any kind he would say that *he* would provide justice, implying he was a better judge than David. (2 Sam. 15:4). In this way, "Absalom stole the hearts of the men of Israel" (2 Sam. 15:6).

After four years of this (some old manuscripts say forty), Absalom was ready to make his move to take over the throne. He went before his father and explained that while he had been in exile at Geshur, he had made a vow to Jehovah to worship Him in Hebron if he was allowed to return to Jerusalem. Now he wanted to go fulfill that vow. This seemed a reasonable request to David, because Absalom had been born in Hebron and was of the tribe of Judah, and he was probably happy to hear of Absalom's religious inclination. Therefore, he told him to go with his blessings.

Absalom could have gone to Hebron without asking his father's permission, but by securing David's approval, the trip could be promoted as a state visit with great fanfare. As part of the preparation, he gathered 200 men from Jerusalem (hand-picked no doubt) who were not in on his plot to go with him to Hebron. He also sent spies, or special messengers, throughout the twelve tribes, preparing the people when they heard the signal to say, "Absalom reigneth in Hebron" (2 Sam. 15:10).

Absalom arrived in Hebron with what must have been an impressive procession and sent for Ahithophel, who lived in Giloh, about seven miles from Hebron. Remember Ahithophel? He was the grandfather of Bathsheba and had been David's most trusted counselor. So highly valued was his advice that men regarded that advice as an oracle of God. After the shameful affair that included the murder of Uriah, Ahithophel had retired in disgust to his native home. Absalom had convinced Ahithophel that he should join in his rebellion, and thus he became the ultimate convert to Absalom's revolt. Daily the number of people pledging themselves to Absalom's cause increased, and the word of his conspiracy came to David in Jerusalem.

DAVID FLEES FROM JERUSALEM

When David heard about Absalom's plot, he decided to vacate Jerusalem, saying to those faithful to him, "Come! We must flee, or none of us will escape from Absalom. We must leave immediately, or he will move quickly to overtake us and bring ruin upon us and put the city to the sword" (2 Sam. 15:14, NIV). We don't know why David was caught so unprepared or why he was so willing to leave Jerusalem without a fight, although his words suggest he feared he couldn't beat Absalom at that point. It does appear he was aware of the plotting against him, for he wrote in Psalm 64:2-4: "Hide me from the secret counsel of the wicked; from the insurrection of the workers of iniquity: who whet their tongue like a sword, and bend their bows to shoot their arrows, even bitter words: that they may shoot in secret at the perfect."

Most likely the reason for David's flight was that Joab and the army directly under him were out of the city. Joab is not heard from until the eighteenth chapter, when those faithful to David took a military stand against Absalom.

Leaving Jerusalem, David's plan was to go east to the fords of the Jordan River and then cross over into the territory of the trans-Jordan tribes, where relative freedom from Absalom's forces would be found. Once there, time could be bought for everyone to think, for tempers to cool, and for calmer heads to prevail. David didn't want to fight his son. He did not wish to see brother against brother, tribe against tribe, Israelite against Israelite. Had he not labored long to unite Israel and to establish a kingdom to the glory of Jehovah?

The fords of the Jordan were about fifteen miles from Jerusalem, not too far for an army used to marching. But for an unprepared host including women and children, it was a long and difficult undertaking that would require a number of rest stops. The flight must have been somewhat haphazard as individuals and groups decided whether to follow David into exile or remain and place themselves under Absalom. So, leaving at different times and from various parts of the city, they all gathered "in a place that was far off" to become properly organized.

The Cherethites and Pelenthites who were the king's bodyguards, and the Gibborim (or Bittites) who had been with David since the days of his youth, would go in front to clear the way, while David, his family, and civilians would come afterward. David took all his family with him except ten concubines who were left behind to care for the palace. As David was checking on who was with him, he spied Ittai the Gittite, who only recently had left Gath and attached himself to David. He must not be confused with Ittai the Benjamite, one of David's mighty men. This Ittai was a Philistine of Gath who not only had accepted David as his king, but had also accepted Jehovah as his God. David, not wanting to impose a life of exile on him, suggested he either go home or remain in Jerusalem. In response, Ittai made a beautiful statement of loyalty: "And Ittai answered the king and said, the Lord liveth, and as my lord the king liveth, surely in what place my lord the king shall be, whether in death or life, even there also will thy servant be" (2 Sam. 15:21). That must have made David's day! Of course he accepted Ittai's confession of loyalty and told him to join his followers.

With much weeping on the part of the people, David and his host left Jerusalem and passed over the brook Kidron. This brook carried off the excess waters from the winter rainy season but was a dry bed most of the year. It separated Jerusalem from Mount Olivet. As David crossed Kidron, the two high priests, Abiathar and Zadok, arrived with the Ark of God and all the Levites. This act of love and loyalty touched David's heart and caused him to utter a truly great statement of resignation to the will of God: "Take the ark of God back into the city. If I find favor in the Lord's eyes, he will bring me back and let me see it and his dwelling place again. But if he says, 'I am not pleased with you,' then I am ready; let him do to me whatever seems good to him" (2 Sam. 15:25-26, NIV). David thus sent the priests and Levites back to the city, but he told them he would wait at the fords of the Jordan for a message from them before crossing the river.

Then David, barefooted, his head covered in full mourning and with a heart pierced with the pain of fleeing from his own son's treachery, climbed the Mount of Olives, weeping with each labored step. In this he foreshadowed Jesus' last walk up the same mountain to the garden of Gethsemane.[1]

David's anguish was increased when one of his messengers told him his wise counselor Ahithophel was among the conspirators with Absalom. David's very human prayer to God was, "O Lord, I pray thee, turn the counsel of Ahithophel into foolishness" (2 Sam. 15:31). Sometimes it seems that it takes forever for God to answer a prayer, but He answered David's immediately by sending Hushai, an elderly friend and counselor of David's, to catch up with the fleeing procession. He came showing mourning, with his coat torn and earth upon his head. He was just the man to counteract Ahithophel's counsel, making it sound foolish to Absalom.

Therefore, David asked his friend to return to the palace and wait for Absalom's entry, then greet Absalom with a pledge to serve him as the new king (2 Sam. 15:34). If Hushai was accepted by Absalom, he would then be in a position to frustrate Ahithophel's advice and to spy for David. Hushai was also told that the two high priests and their sons were on their side, and that he could send messages by them. So Hushai returned and arrived as Absalom was entering the city.

Certainly this plot to deceive Absalom was not proper by the letter of the law. However, don't you hope the plot works?

At the top of the Mount of Olives, David stopped for worship. According to Jewish sources, while there he wrote the third psalm, which is a prayer of great faith even when all seemed to be crumbling around him. The first two verses present an accurate picture of David's condition in the eyes of many: "Lord, how are they increased that trouble me! Many are they that rise up against me. Many there be which say of my soul, There is no help for him in God." But David's view of his condition was quite different, as presented in verses 3-6: "But thou, O Lord, art a shield for me; my glory, and the lifter up of mine head. I cried unto the Lord with my voice, and he heard me out of his holy hill. Selah. I laid me down and slept; I awaked; for the Lord sustained me. I will not be afraid of ten thousands of people, that have set themselves against me round about."

The expression of David that God was "the lifter up of mine head" is so precious and so true of the God-David, Father-son relationship. The son is depressed, and his head is bowed in sorrow or shame. Then the father comes along and lifts the son's head with his hands, looks into his eyes with loving confidence, and says, "Everything will work out well" (see Rom. 8:28).

The sustenance gained by David from the Lord through faith enabled him to lie down, sleep, and awaken, refreshed even in the most trying of times. How much better this was for him than to lie awake, tossing and turning with worry! "Humble yourselves therefore under the mighty hand of God, that he may exalt you in due time: casting all your care upon him; for he careth for you" (1 Peter 5:6-7).

Psalm 4 seems to be a shadow of the third psalm. Possibly it was written at a later date by David for use in public worship, because it was given to the chief musician. Compare verse 8 to verse 5 in Psalm 3: "I will lie down and sleep in peace, for you alone, O Lord make me dwell in safety" (NIV). Consider also the excellent counsel of verse 5: "Offer the sacrifices of righteousness, and put your trust in the Lord."

When David had started down the other side of the Mount of Olives, he met Ziba, the servant of the crippled Mephibosheth. Ziba had come with two asses for members of the king's household to ride upon, as well as a load of food and medicinal supplies. At first glance, this seemed to be a thoughtful gesture. David asked where Mephibosheth was, and Ziba replied that he had remained in Jerusalem, thinking he would be made king in place of his father, Saul (2 Sam. 16:3).

Why would Mephibosheth think Absalom would relinquish the throne to him? It would have been an absurd thought if Mephibosheth had entertained it, but he had not. It was all a despicable lie manufactured by the wicked Ziba. Later, in 2 Samuel 19:26, we find that Ziba had told Mephibosheth he would saddle an ass for him to ride on so they could flee with David. But Ziba left him behind, and Mephibosheth was so upset that he did not take care of his injured feet, trim his beard, or wash his clothes from that day until David returned to Jerusalem. However, not knowing that Ziba was lying, David did not question Ziba's word but rather said to him, "All that belonged to Mephibosheth is now yours" (2 Sam. 16:4, NIV). On David's part this was a rash decision, and on Ziba's part it was a dangerous game to take sides with David, for if David was defeated, his gift to Ziba would mean nothing. But evidently Ziba thought David would win back the throne.

Later, when David did return to Jerusalem, he learned the truth and ordered Mephibosheth and Ziba to divide the land he had hastily given to Ziba. But the unselfish son of Jonathan was so happy to see David back in Jerusalem victoriously that he said, "Let [Ziba] take everything, now that my lord the king has arrived home safely" (2 Sam. 19:30, NIV). It appears there may have been more to the story of Ziba than is recorded in the Bible.

Emotionally, it had been an up-and-down journey for David as various people reacted to his flight. Some, as have been mentioned, showed great loyalty, and some had betrayed him, but in the story of Shimei we have the ultimate reproach to David. As David and his host trudged on toward the Jordan, there appeared a man of the house of Saul on the hillside above them at Bahurim, who cursed David and pelted both him and his servants with stones. Shimei was the man's name, and he must have been a fanatic to do what he did with the King's guards all around. He called David a man of blood and said God was punishing him for all he had done to the family of Saul (2 Sam. 16:7-8).

Abishai, the brother of Joab, asked the king's permission to lop the head off the "dead dog" that dared to curse the king. But David, resigned to his fate, said Shimei's curses might be God's will. David must have reasoned that if he could stand the pain of having his own son seek his life, he could certainly stand a cursing from a Benjamite. Maybe if he could accept in the proper spirit the wrongs being done to him that day, Jehovah would repay him with good. "So David and his men continued along the road while Shimei was going along the hillside opposite him, cursing as he went and throwing stones at him and showering him with dirt" (2 Sam. 16:13).

At last David and those with him arrived at the fords of the Jordan, tired to the bone. They made camp and refreshed themselves, while back at the palace, Hushai was greeting Absalom. Absalom replied, "Is this thy kindness to thy friend? why wentest thou not with thy friend?" (2 Sam. 16:17). Absalom of all people should have been acutely aware of the fickleness of so-called friends. Only in God can we put our trust and never be betrayed. But Hushai assured Absalom he would serve him because he was chosen by "the Lord, and this people, and all the men of Israel" (2 Sam. 16:18).

ABSALOM IN JERUSALEM

The question now in Absalom's mind, which he put to Ahithophel, was what should be done to secure their victory. Ahithophel offered two suggestions: First, Absalom should sleep with his father's concubines whom he had left to take care of the palace. Then all Israel would know he had antagonized his father irredeemably. Second, he asked for 12,000 men with whom to pursue David immediately. "I will come upon him while he is weary and weak handed" (2 Sam. 17:2). He would kill only the king, but bring all the people back to Absalom.

Ahithophel must have had a great personal hatred toward David to propose such a plan, which Absalom and the elders of Israel with him accepted.

A tent was pitched on the very roof where David had first been tempted to seduce Bathsheba, and Absalom "went in unto his father's concubines in the sight of all Israel" (2 Sam. 16:22). Remember that God had said to David through the prophet Nathan, "you did it in secret, but I will do this thing in broad daylight before all Israel" (2 Sam. 12:12, NIV). How did this revolting action strengthen the hands of Absalom's followers? W. J. Deane suggests in his commentary that when Absalom thus made the breach between himself and David irreconcilable, Absalom's supporters no longer had to concern themselves with the possibility, however remote, of a joint reign of father and son.

It should be noted that in that day, women were treated as the personal property of men, with no say about the misuse of their bodies. All women should be thankful for the freedom and equality that are theirs by the application of principles laid down by Christ.

As for the second part of Ahithophel's plan, before placing him at the head of a hastily organized military expedition, Absalom called for Hushai to secure a second opinion. Maybe he felt a little jealous of the attention and honor Ahithophel was receiving. Regardless, Hushai immediately contradicted the counsel of Ahithophel and keyed his appeal to Absalom's vanity. He reminded Absalom of the experience and bravery of his father and his mighty men saying, "They are fighters and as fierce as a wild bear robbed of her cubs" (v. 8). Hushai continued to reason that David would not be found out in the open, waiting to be taken, but would already be hidden in a cave. There would be a battle, he said, and Ahithophel and his army would suffer such losses that the hearts of even the brave of Israel would melt with fear of David and his men.

"What you need to do," Hushai counseled Absalom, "is take time to gather a huge army from every part of Israel. Then, with you yourself leading them, you can attack David in force. Not one of his men will survive" (see 2 Sam. 17:7-12). The advice sounded so good that Absalom and all his advisers chose to follow it. "For the Lord had appointed to defeat the good counsel of Ahithophel, to the intent that the Lord might bring evil upon Absalom" (2 Sam. 17:14).

Hushai, not being in Absalom's inner council and not knowing he had succeeded in frustrating Ahithophel's counsel, passed the word to Zadok and Abiathar to tell David not to tarry at the brink of the Jordan but, by all means, to cross over before he and those with him were swallowed.

During this period, David wrote Psalm 55, in which he had this to say about Ahithophel:

If an enemy were insulting me, I could endure it;
if a foe were raising himself against me, I could hide
    from him.
But it is you, a man like myself, my companion, my close
    friend,
with whom I once enjoyed sweet fellowship as we walked
    with the throng at the house of God. . . .
My companion attacks his friends; he violates his covenant.
His speech is smooth as butter, yet war is in his heart;
his words are more soothing than oil, yet they are drawn
    swords. (vv. 12-14, 20-21, NIV)

Ahithophel found, as did Judas and many other traitors, that the road of a betrayer is difficult. When his counsel was rejected, he went home, settled his affairs, and hanged himself (2 Sam. 17:23).

David, on the other hand, imagined a different kind of escape from shame: "Oh, that I had the wings of a dove! I would fly away and be at rest" (Psa. 55:6, NIV). Who at times has not been disillusioned with those around him and wished for the wings of a bird so he might fly away to some restful utopia? Jesus offers us rest if we learn to be like Him (Matt. 11:28-30). David also knew the key to spiritual rest and expressed it in verse 22: "Cast thy burden upon the Lord, and he shall sustain thee."

Psalm 41, although it may have been written at a later time, is also relevant. Verse nine is certainly about Ahithophel: "Yea, mine own familiar friend, in whom I trusted, which did eat of my bread, hath lifted up his heel against me." Jesus quoted this verse in John 13:18 as a reference to Judas.

David and all those with him crossed the Jordan as advised and proceeded to Mahanaim, a prominent and fortified city in Gilead. Three of the chieftains of the area placed themselves at David's call and furnished him and his people with food and supplies. Their actions showed their love for David and their courage.

During the next three months, those who composed David's army grew into the thousands. Absalom had been anointed king in Jerusalem and had also gathered a huge army over which he placed Amasa, a cousin to Joab and Abhishai and a nephew to David. God's statement that David's problems would arise from within his family was proven to be accurate.

PSALMS OF DAVID'S FLIGHT

Since David's habit was to pour out his fears and cries for God's help in psalms, it's not surprising that he wrote at least nine psalms during his flight from Absalom, making it one of his most productive writing periods. The major themes of his psalms of this period were for God to have mercy and save him; that God was his sustainer, shield and refuge; and that in God he placed his trust.

In Psalm 143 David pleaded not only his case but the case of humanity when he sought mercy rather than justice from God.

> "Do not bring your servant into judgment,
> For no one living is righteous before you."
> (v. 2, NIV)

Paul agreed with David in Romans 3:23 by saying, "All have sinned, and come short of the glory of God."

David told God his enemies had crushed him to the ground, and, therefore, his heart was desolate until he remembered "the days of old" and meditated on all God had done for him and his forefathers. To recall God's past mercies made David thirst after the Lord as the dry, weary land longs for rain. "I stretch forth my hands unto thee ... hear me speedily, O Lord," pleaded David. Thus begins one of the most poignant prayers ever offered:

> "Cause me to hear thy loving-kindness in the
>   morning; for in thee do I trust:
> cause me to know the way wherein I should walk;
>   for I lift up my soul unto thee.
> Deliver me, O Lord, from mine enemies:

I flee unto thee to hide me.
Teach me to do thy will;
   for thou art my God: thy Spirit is good;
lead me into the land of uprightness.
Quicken me, O Lord, for thy name's sake:
   for thy righteousness' sake bring my soul
     out of trouble.
. . . for I am thy servant."

              (vv. 8-12, emphasis added)

How very child-like was this prayer of the 62-year-old David.

Verse 4 of Psalm 70 remains a gem for us today:

"Let all those that seek thee rejoice and be
   glad in thee:
And let such as love thy salvation say continually,
Let God be magnified."

In Psalm 62, David teaches that only in God can we place our trust, because he has all power but yet is full of mercy. Trust must not be placed in our own selves or in other persons, great or small or in power over others or in riches.

Putting Truth into Action

1. David apparently knew of Absalom's plotting yet did nothing to stop it. Do you agree or disagree with that approach? Why? What lessons should we draw from this as people in positions of responsibility in church or on the job?
2. David was deeply distressed by the treason of Ahithophel. What principles might we learn from

that story about how we treat people and whom to trust?

3. How can we avoid making bad decisions under stress like the one David made concerning Ziba and Mephibosheth?

4. Can you think of a possible time today when it would be proper to use deception to foil an evil plot as David did through Hushai?

5. Why do you think David was so loved by God?

CHAPTER 11

Blinded by Love

2 Samuel 18 and 19

The love of parents for their children is amazing. It's so strong that a father will disregard his own safety to rush into a burning home in an effort to save his baby. It's so warm that a mother will deny herself needed clothes in order to buy a party dress for her teenage daughter.

Unfortunately, parental love sometimes gets distorted into being "blind." Wanting to believe the best about their children, parents can block out and refuse to face the shortcomings and problems of their kids. "Even when confronted with incontrovertible evidence, [parents] will deny that their son or daughter is on drugs or into any other trouble," writes minister and author Stephen Brown. "Time after time, when the parents of convicted criminals are asked about their children, they reply, 'He's such a good boy. He's never done anything really bad. I can't believe they're talking about my son.' "

David seems to have suffered from this kind of blindness regarding Absalom. And in the final conflict with this traitorous son, David let his personal feelings undermine his judgment. That's bad for anyone, but it's especially bad for a leader.

Thus, looking at this episode in David's life gives us a stark lesson in the danger of making unwise decisions in times of personal distress. We also see further into the heart of the man and the deep reservoir of faith from which he drew—and from which we can, too.

ABSALOM'S DEATH AND DAVID'S GRIEF

Having had time to regroup and being joined by Joab, David divided his army into three divisions. Joab, Ittai the Gittite, and Abishai were placed over them. David planned personally to lead his three armies into battle, but his men prevailed on him to remain in the fortified city of Mahanaim. Before the armies departed the city, he gave clear orders to the three commanders, in the presence of the troops, to deal gently with Absalom.

After having crossed the Jordan, the army of Absalom was lured into battle in the dense forest of Ephraim, where sheer numbers of men were not nearly so important as stealth and strategy. The hastily collected army of Israel was no match in hand-to-hand combat for David's experienced men. In addition, the forest itself devoured more men than were slain by the sword. The steep slopes, with perilous pits and sudden cliffs, were difficult enough for the trained and dedicated soldier; for Absalom's unpaid volunteers, they proved impossible.

Separated and disorganized, the army of Absalom melted from around him, and he found himself alone except for scouts from David's army. (We must wonder where Amasa was during this battle.) The newly anointed king plunged madly into a forest

thicket on mule-back, his beautiful, long hair stream-
ing behind him. "The mule went under the thick
boughs of a great oak, and his head caught hold of
the oak, and he was taken up between the heaven
and the earth; and the mule that was under him
went away" (2 Sam. 18:9). Nowhere in the inspired
record of this incident are we told that Absalom's
hair got caught in the tree's branches. The writer
calls attention to this only because from childhood
it was heard that Absalom's hair caught in the
branches, when in fact that's wholly an assumption.
It is so easy to accept assumptions as factual.

As Absalom was hanging from the tree, one of
David's soldiers saw his plight and reported it to
Joab, who asked him, "Why didn't you kill him? I
would have rewarded you well." The soldier replied
that for no amount would he have dared to lay a
hand on Absalom, because he had heard David's
command. An irritated Joab, fearing Absalom might
disentangle himself and escape, grabbed three darts,
or spears, and rushed to where Absalom was hanging. He drove the spears through Absalom's heart.
Then the ten young men who carried Joab's armor
encircled Absalom and completed the job.

Joab wasn't bloodthirsty, and he didn't lightly
disobey David's order. Rather, he saw the execution
as an action necessary to end the rebellion and bring
a return to peace among the tribes and families of
all Israel. His action was also more in keeping with
the law of Moses than David's intended leniency
(see Deut. 21:21). Once Absalom was dead, Joab
stopped his army from pursuing the army of Israel.
The rebellion was over, and there was no need for
further bloodshed.

Absalom's body was taken down, thrown into a pit, and covered with stones until a great heap was raised over him. This monument of shame was vastly different from the vain monument Absalom had built for himself in the king's dale (2 Sam. 18:18). It is not within the ability of man to judge himself. Wouldn't we all like to write our own epitaphs? However, those around us will compose our real epitaphs, and finally and eternally God will seal our lives.

With the rebellion over, the news of the outcome would have to be sent to David, who was anxiously waiting at the gates of Mahanaim. Ahimaaz, the fleet-footed son of Zadok, wanted to deliver what he considered the good news of a providential victory, but Joab, knowing the news would be both good and bad to David, refused to let Ahimaaz be the messenger. Instead he chose a man simply called "the Cushite" to go. A messenger of good news was often rewarded generously, but the bearer of bad news might be killed. Joab did not wish to endanger the son of the high priest, but a man from Ethiopia was thought expendable.

Receiving his instructions, the Cushite bowed to Joab and took off running, but Ahimaaz, filled with youthful zeal, again pleaded for permission to go. Joab warned him, but he would not listen to reason; finally, Joab granted him permission. Ahimaaz ran on the more level plain and arrived at Mahanaim before the Cushite. From the city's watchtower, the two runners were seen by the watchman, who reported to David that Ahimaaz was first. David said, "He is a good man. He comes with good news." Ahimaaz, running toward the king, called out, "All is well!" After bowing before the king, he continued,

"Praise be to the Lord your God! He has delivered up the men who lifted their hands against my lord the king" (2 Sam. 18:28, NIV).

Without a thank you to God or man, David asked, "Is the young man Absalom safe?" Only then did Ahimaaz understand why Joab had warned him that the father's love was stronger than patriotism or victory. What to say? Ahimaaz made a lie rather than break the bad news to David, saying he saw a great confusion just as Joab was about to send him but didn't know what it was (2 Sam. 18:29). David then told Ahimaaz to stand aside to make room for the second runner. As soon as the Cushite had also announced the victory, David asked about Absalom again. This messenger indicated he was dead.

David was shaken. One is never ready for the death of a loved one. He went to his room and wept, and as he went he agonized, "O my son Absalom, my son, my son Absalom! Would God I had died for thee, O Absalom, my son, my son!" (2 Sam. 18:33).[1]

David had now lost three sons. The self-guilt must have weighed heavily on his heart. His grief was so great that it changed what should have been a day of celebration for a victorious deliverance into a day of shame.

As David's weary armies came back into the city, they were welcomed not by hugs and kisses, but by the sounds of the mourning David, who was letting his feelings overturn his sense of responsibility. They felt let down by the king and did not understand. Kings and leaders were and still are not acceptable leaders if they show personal emotion to the detriment of their followers. We expect our leaders to put aside personal feelings for the good of the people, and so did they.

So when Joab was told of David's reaction, he correctly went to the king, rebuked him, and told him to pull himself together, saying,

> Today you have humiliated all your men, who have just saved your life and the lives of your sons and daughters and the lives of your wives and concubines. You love those who hate you and hate those who love you. You have made it clear today that the commanders and their men mean nothing to you. I see that you would be pleased if Absalom were alive today and all of us were dead. Now go out and encourage your men. I swear by the Lord that if you don't go out, not a man will be left with you by nightfall. This will be worse for you than all the calamities that have come upon you from your youth till now. (2 Sam. 19:5-7, NIV)

David did not enjoy Joab's stinging speech, but he knew it was true; therefore, he went out and did his official duty of greeting the troops.[2]

The Call to Return

Elsewhere in Israel, as the remaining soldiers of Absalom's army arrived home from the battle, they discussed the state of affairs one with another. Even though many were unhappy with David, they had to admit he had made Israel strong and was a dependable leader. The desire for his restoration to the throne became general, so messages from the leaders of the various tribes began to arrive at David's door in Mahanaim, asking him to return to Jerusalem and resume his duties as king of Israel. Only the tribe of Judah held back. This must have been a cross for David to bear, because he wrote about Judah's hesitation in Psalm 69: "I am become a stranger unto my brethren, and an alien unto my mother's children. For the zeal of thine house hath eaten me up; and the reproaches of them that reproached thee are fallen upon me" (vv. 8-9).[3]

Psalm 69 is messianic not only in verse nine, but also in verse 21, which reads, "They gave me also gall for my meat; and in my thirst they gave me vinegar to drink." The details of David's prophecy were fulfilled at the death of Christ and recorded in Matthew 27:34 and John 19:29-30.

In the twenty-eighth verse David refers to the "book of life" that contains the names of the righteous. This holy book is mentioned four other times in the Old Testament and six times in the New Testament. We must live in such a way as to assure that our names are not "blotted out of the book of life" because as David wrote, "O God, thou knowest my foolishness; and my sins are not hid from thee" (Psa. 69:5).

David sent to Zadok and Abiathar, asking them to intercede with the leaders of the tribe of Judah on his behalf. He said to tell them, "Ye are my brethren, ye are my bone and my flesh: wherefore then are ye the last to bring back the king?" (2 Sam. 19:12). He then promised to make Amasa captain of the host in the place of Joab. This last message smacks of Politics 101. Why would he make such a promise to Amasa unless it was to gain his support? David's plan worked! The people of Judah unanimously sent word inviting him back to the throne.

PSALMS OF GILEAD

Along with Psalm 69 the following psalms are assigned to the time when David was in Mahanaim.

Psalm 5 is a prayer asking for the defeat of the wicked and for protection for the righteous. Verse 8 gives David's prayer, which might well be ours also: "Lead me, O Lord in thy righteousness, because of mine enemies; make thy way straight before my face." Psalm 38 sounds as if it were written by Job, but it is ascribed to David in the title and must have been written at some time during this period of harassment. It is a pitiful cry for help by a penitent David who was suffering severe physical ailments:

"O Lord, rebuke me not in thy wrath:
Neither chasten me in thy hot displeasure.
For thine arrows stick fast in me,
and thy hand presseth me sore.
There is no soundness in my flesh because of thine
   anger;
Neither is there any rest in my bones because of my sin.
For mine iniquities are gone over mine head;
as a heavy burden they are too heavy for me.
My wounds stink and are corrupt,
because of my foolishness.
I am troubled; I am bowed down greatly;
I go mourning all the day long.
For my loins are filled with a loathsome disease:
and there is no soundness in my flesh.
I am feeble and sore broken:
I have roared by reason of the disquietness of my heart."

(vv. 1-8, Am.T.)

The Psalm ends with this plea:

> "Forsake me not, O Lord: O my God,
>   be not far from me
> Make haste to help me,
>   O Lord my salvation"
>
>   (vv. 21-22)

Sometimes even a saint is depressed and despondent with life, yet he does not wish to say anything rash in public that enemies of the Lord may use destructively. The saint feels, however, that he must "let off steam," so he does it in prayer to the Lord. That is what Psalm 39 is about. David was casting his cares on God, as we're told to do in 1 Peter 5:7. Such a prayer can bring relief to a troubled mind, even as it seemed to bring relief to David at a time when he felt disciplined by and a stranger to God.

David had been a man of purpose and drive, a goal-oriented person, but the tumult surrounding Absalom's rebellion had caused him to see the absolute frailty and vanity of life. This realization fell so crushingly upon him that he could see that the beauty of life is like the all-too-brief beauty of a moth (v. 11). If that were the case, he reasoned, what has a person left to look forward to? "And now, Lord, what wait I for? My hope is in thee" (v. 7).

David has, in other meditative psalms, written of God's knowledge of him before he was ever formed or born. Now he wished God to reveal his future to him: "Lord, make me to know mine end, and the measure of my days, what it is" (v. 4). The psalm closes with a plea for an answer (vv. 12-13).

Psalm 40 appears to be the follow-up to Psalm 39. God had heard David's cry and delivered him out of the pit of despair:

I waited patiently for the Lord
And he inclined unto me, and heard my cry.
He brought me up also out of a horrible pit,
    out of the miry clay,
and set my feet upon a rock, and established my goings.
And he hath put a new song in my mouth,
    even praise unto our God:
many shall see it, and fear,
and shall trust in the Lord (vv. 1-3).

E. R. Conder said, "Trouble impoverishes the children of this world, but enriches the children of God." The new song of which Psalm 40:3 and Revelation 5:9-10 speak is one the heart must learn in the school of trials. It is a song of deliverance. O, that we might understand that deliverance and escape are not synonymous! A prisoner might file through the bars of his cell and escape, but the prisoner who is pardoned by the governor is delivered. The new song is a song of unmerited forgiveness. It is a song of love and praise, praise of God's compassionate grace. It is a song of deepened experience, of an enriched spiritual life with a wiser, stronger, and humbler faith. He who has been first in the pit of despair, then on his knees in prayer, then on the rock of faith is the person who will stand and sing praise to God.

David would have named the wondrous works of God, but they are beyond numbering; therefore, he concentrated on the greatest blessing, mercy. God's merciful grace is not obtained, he wrote, by sacrifices and legalistic offerings, but by the complete devotion

of one's self to obeying God's law and openly praising the Lord (vv. 5-10). David realized that even
though God had delivered him from the pit, he was
still surrounded by innumerable evils. Therefore,
he continued to need the Lord's tender mercies
(vv. 11-16).

The psalm closes with the marvelous statement
that even though a person be poor and needy, the
Lord's thoughts are upon that one individual (v.
17). That statement, more than any other, illustrates
the infinite care of the Lord for each of us.

Putting Truth into Action

1. What are the dangers in being blind to a loved
one's sins and shortcomings over a long period of
time?
2. When David's army returned from battle, he needed
to set aside his grief temporarily for the sake of his
followers. Do parents sometimes need to do the
same for the sake of their children? If so, under
what circumstances?
3. Why is it that we sometimes get the least respect
from our own families, just as David's tribe of Judah
was the last to invite him back to the throne? How
do we earn respect of those closest to us?
4. What is the danger in Bible study of accepting
as factual an assumption? Give some examples.
5. Discuss Psalms 39 and 40.

CHAPTER 12

Living Well, Finishing Well

2 Samuel 23
1 Chronicles 22, 28 and 29
1 Kings 1 and 2

Perhaps you've heard the stereotype that says old age somehow magically transforms people into sweet, grandmotherly types. Don't believe it. Advanced age doesn't generally change people at all—they just become more of what they've been making themselves into all their lives. Sweet people do become sweeter, but bitter folks grow even more bitter.

David, too, became more of what he had always been. And there was no defeatism in him as he lived his final years and prepared for death. He proceeded as he always had—with purpose, energy (almost to the very end), and reliance on God. In this, too, he provides us a model.

As author Stuart Briscoe observed: "David spent his last days absorbed with his project [gathering the materials with which Solomon would build the temple]. Not only that, he gathered the future leaders of the nation together and talked to them about running things after he was gone. And he sought to prepare Solomon, who would be king in his place. It was very obvious. His heart was burning for his God, and he was eager to see the spark ignite in the hearts of the leaders who would carry the torch after he was gone. . . .

"Let me urge you to decide in your heart today that you will maintain an active and aggressive walk with the Lord in your later years. It may be that your richest years of service to Christ and His church lie ahead of you! Remember, there is no such thing as being a retired overcomer" (David: A Heart for God, pp. 162, 163).

THE BEGINNING OF THE END

David and those who had so sorrowfully gone with him to Mahanaim left victoriously and marched to the Jordan, where they were met by the men of Judah and escorted over the river and back to Jerusalem. The time for David was late; he was well into the sixty-second year of his life and the thirty-second year of his reign.

But even before David had crossed the Jordan, Shimei and Ziba, those two slimy characters of the tribe of Benjamin, came before him. They were at the head of a thousand men of their tribe. Shimei came to plead for his life, and Ziba came, most likely, to remind David of the promise he had made concerning Mephibosheth's property. David could not easily afford to offend the tribe of Benjamin at that delicate time, so he made another compromise that was probably ill-advised in the long run. He promised Shimei, "Thou shalt not die" (2 Sam. 19:23). If David didn't regret making that promise at the time, he most certainly regretted it later, and he advised Solomon, when he ascended the throne, to execute Shimei (1 Kings 2:8-9).

The eighty-year-old Barzillai, who had provided food for David and his company while at Mahanaim, crossed the river with his friend David. The king invited him to continue with him to Jerusalem and become a part of his court, but Barzillai excused himself due to the infirmities of age and his desire to die at home. However, it was arranged for David to take Chimham, probably Barzillai's son with him. David kissed the aged man and blessed him as they parted (2 Sam. 19:31-39). How sadly sweet it is to part with friends, knowing that, not in this world but in a better one, we will again embrace.

David's return trip to Jerusalem was monopolized by the men of Judah even though they were the last tribe to invite him back. This caused the other tribes to complain to David. Fierce words were exchanged between the men of Judah and the men of ten tribes. (One tribe was missing in this dispute, but which one is not mentioned.)

The tribe not involved was certainly not Benjamin, because a traitor named Sheba, the son of Bichri, a Benjamite, appeared on the scene and incited the men of Israel to another rebellion against David. Apparently, the nation's new unity wasn't very strong. "So all the men of Israel deserted David to follow Sheba son of Bichri. But the men of Judah stayed by their king all the way from the Jordan to Jerusalem" (2 Sam. 20:2, NIV). Thus, the end of one rebellion spawned yet another.

After David had set the palace in order, he gave an order to his newly appointed commander, Amasa, to assemble the fighting men at Judah and bring them to him in three days. But the three days passed, and Amasa had not yet appeared. David was then forced to fall back on Abishai for he feared that unless Sheba was stopped quickly, he might do more harm to the kingdom than did Absalom.

Upon receiving the king's orders, Abishai took off after Sheba with the Cherethites, the Pelethites, and all the mighty men, including the demoted Joab. When they got to Gibeon, some ten miles north of Jerusalem, Amasa came to meet them. Joab met Amasa with a false show of friendship, then used a trick to kill him with one blow of the sword. The army then followed Joab, in pursuit of Sheba (2 Sam. 20:4-13).

Joab and Abishai finally trapped Sheba in the fortified city of Abel of Bethmaachah, which was located in the far northern district of the northern tribe of Naphtali. Joab was proceeding with full military effort to throw the city's wall down when a wise woman of the city called for a conference. Joab assured her he had no desire to destroy the city but was only after the traitorous Sheba. "Hand over this one man," Joab said, "and I'll withdraw from the city." Her replay was, "His head will be thrown to you from the wall" (2 Sam. 20:21, NIV). Sheba's head was thrown down, so Joab sent the men of Judah home and returned to Jerusalem to serve the king, once again as commander of the host of Israel.

For whatever reason, David did not or perhaps could not discipline Joab for murdering Amasa. But later he advised Solomon, "Do . . . not let his [gray] head go down to the grave in peace" (1 Kings 2:6). Solomon, following David's advice, had Joab executed.

The wise woman of Abel, on the other hand, receives high praise from a number of commentators as a peacemaker. But it seems that her method of peacemaking, killing the troublemaker, was not exactly what Christ had in mind when He said, "Blessed are the peacemakers: for they shall be called the children of God" (Matt. 5:9).

Following the end of Sheba's rebellion, the last years of David's reign were peaceful both without and within Israel. David concentrated on three things: (1) preparing the materials with which Solomon would build the Lord's temple; (2) organizing the religious, military, and civil officers of the state; and (3) preparing Solomon for the throne and the leaders of the nation to accept and support him.

In 1 Chronicles 23-26, the organization of the priests and Levites is given. The military and civil organization is given in 2 Samuel 20:23-26 and in 1 Chronicles 27. David's ability to organize and delegate has already been noted. No one can completely assess David as a leader without recognizing this essential talent.

The first mention of the position of superintendent of forced labor, or "men subject to task work," is found in 2 Samuel 20:24 (see the NIV, ASV, NASB). This officer supplied the work force for the colossal building programs of David and Solomon in Jerusalem, including the temple and palaces. The men compelled to labor may at first have been only the descendants of the native Palestinians, but later the work force was expanded to include Israelites who fell behind on their ever increasing taxes. This program of oppression increasingly became a cause of complaint and eventually the chief cause of the division of the kingdom under Solomon's son Rehoboam (1 Kings 12:3-20).

DAVID PREPARES FOR THE FUTURE

David's desire to praise God above all is manifested in his concept of the temple to be built for Jehovah. He envisioned that it "must be exceeding [magnificent], of fame and of glory throughout all countries" (1 Chron. 22:5).[1]

Knowing Solomon was "young and tender," David exercised great care in instructing Solomon in the importance of constructing the Lord's house. He gave him elaborate and precise plans for every part of the temple and its furnishings, saying, "All this is in writing, . . . because the hand of the Lord was upon me, and he gave me understanding in all the details of the plan" (1 Chron. 28:19, NIV). F. Whitfield wrote in *The Pulpit Commentary*, "Solomon could not lay a single stone, nor make a single beam, not deviate one hair's breadth from this pattern thus handed to him. The Lord himself is the architect of his own house, whether it be the tabernacle, temple, the Church of Christ, or in a man's soul" (see 1 Cor. 3:16). We have no right to deviate in any way whatsoever from any divine pattern given to us in the Bible.

Then David gave Solomon a charge that's applicable to every young person today:

And thou, Solomon my son, know thou the God of thy father, and serve him with a perfect heart and with a willing mind; for the Lord searcheth all hearts, and understandeth all the imaginations of the thought: if thou seek him, he will be found of thee; but if thou forsake him, he will cast thee off for ever. . . . Be strong and of good courage, and do it: fear not, nor be dismayed: for the Lord God, even my God, will be with thee; he will not fail thee, nor forsake thee (1 Chron. 28:9-20).

Notice the personal relationship of David to Jehovah when he referred to Him as "even my God." David did walk and talk with God as a friend.

Next David called for an assembly of all the officials throughout Israel in Jerusalem. In his address to the assembly, he told of his desire to build a "house of rest for the ark of the covenant of the Lord, and for the footstool of our God" (1 Chron. 28:2), but that God would not allow him to do so because he was a man of war and had shed blood. He reviewed how he had been chosen by God from all his father's sons to be king, and he explained that God had now chosen Solomon to be his successor on the throne. Then he charged Israel to observe God's will that it might be well with them. It was probably at this time that Solomon was first anointed king.

David went on to tell the assembly that Solomon was young and inexperienced and therefore would need the help of everyone. He said he had amassed great treasures toward the building of the temple and was giving gold and silver of his own fortune for the project. He called upon the leaders to give also: "Who is willing to consecrate himself today to the Lord?" (1 Chron. 29:5, NIV) The leaders of Israel responded with generosity, and the people rejoiced, for their leaders "had given freely and wholeheartedly to the Lord. David the king also rejoiced greatly" (1 Chron. 29:9, NIV).[2]

David blessed Jehovah before the assembly with this psalm:

Praise be to you, O Lord, God of our father Israel, from everlasting to everlasting. Yours, O Lord, is the

Praise be to you, O Lord, God of our father Israel,
from everlasting to everlasting. Yours, O Lord, is the
greatness and the power and the glory and the
majesty and the splendor, for everything in heaven
and earth is yours.

Yours, O Lord, is the kingdom; you are exalted as
head over all.

In your hands are strength and power to exalt and
give strength to all.

Now, our God, we give you thanks, and praise your
glorious name.

(1 Chron. 29:10-13, NIV)

David then acknowledged that in their giving to
God, they were only giving to Him that which was
already His (1 Chron. 29:14). When we give to the
Lord, we likewise need to remember we are only
returning to God a portion of the riches He has given
us.

On the day following the assembly, a thousand
bulls and a thousand rams and a thousand male
lambs were sacrificed to the Lord, together with
drink offerings and other sacrifices. "They ate and
drank with great joy in the presence of the Lord
that day. Then they acknowledged Solomon son of
David as king a second time, anointing him before
the Lord to be ruler and Zadok to be priest? (1 Chron.
29:22, NIV).

THREE GREAT PSALMS

In the days, maybe years, following the assembly,
David continued to reign, with the teenage Solomon
waiting for the "changing of the guard." In this
period, David wrote three of his greatest psalms.

Psalm 37 is called the "Fret Not Psalm," because David used the term three times (in vv. 1, 7, and 8). It is a didactic poem written in David's old age: "I have been young, and now I am old; yet have I not seen the righteous forsaken, nor his seed begging bread" (v. 25). The psalm was written to reassure us when we are disturbed by the frequent prosperity of the wicked. So often we're discouraged because the openly wicked seem to have everything, while the innocent and righteous seem to go unrewarded. David said not to be angry and fretful about this injustice, because fretting "leads only to evil" (v. 8, NIV). Rather, we should "trust in the Lord, and do good" (v. 3). This psalm teaches that the wicked will inevitably be destroyed, while the righteous will be saved.

This psalm could also be called the "wait for the Lord Psalm," because David encouraged us three times to wait patiently for Jehovah (in v. 7, 9, and 34). We are prone to be so impatient, because we tend to think only of this lifetime, while God considers eternity.

In verse 4 David said: "Delight yourself also in the Lord; and he shall give thee the desires of thine heart." If we truly find pleasure in right living and happiness in worshiping God, He will bless us. Note that the verse does not say we should find delight in the desires of our hearts, but rather in the desires of the Lord. If we find delight in the Lord, the desires of our hearts will be pure.

"The mouth of the righteous man utters wisdom, and his tongue speaks what is just. The law of his God is in his heart; his feet do not slip" (vv. 30-31, NIV). What keeps the feet of the righteous from slipping? The Word of God does, because it guides and motivates the righteous.

Three thousand years have passed since David penned Psalm 139. "Such knowledge is too wonderful for me; it is high, I cannot attain unto it" (v. 6). God's infinite knowledge and omnipresence as described in this psalm far exceed our ability to comprehend.

David acknowledged that God knew him even before he was formed in his mother's womb: "All the days ordained for me were written in your book before one of them came to be" (v. 16, NIV).[3] "I will praise thee; for I am fearfully and wonderfully made" (v. 14). Any examination of our bodies, much less our minds, testifies to the truth of David's words and to the fact that we were intelligently and purposely designed rather than blindly and accidentally made, as evolutionists would have us believe.

"Marvelous are thy works; and that my soul knoweth right well" (v. 14). After a lifetime of close association with the Lord, David was well aware of the wonderful works of Jehovah. The marvelous thing about David was that after that life of association with the Lord, the wisdom of God was still precious and inexhaustible to him. Once the noted Bible scholar H. Leo Boles was heard to say, "After sixty years of Bible reading, I never read a chapter of God's Word without getting a meaning or thought from it that I have never gotten before." That can be said by us today, *if* we work to stay close to the Lord. Truly, the riches in the Bible cannot be exhausted.

In relatively few words, David also made one of the best-ever statements of God's omnipresence, which we do well to remember:

> Whither shall I go from thy Spirit?
> Or whither shall I flee from thy presence?
> If I ascend up into heaven, thou art there:
> if I make my bed in hell, behold, thou art there.
> If I take the wings of the morning,
> and dwell in the uttermost parts of the sea;
> Even there shall thy hand lead me,
> and thy right hand shall hold me.
> If I say, Surely the darkness shall cover me;
> Even the night shall be light about me.
> Yea, the darkness hideth not from thee;
> but the night shineth as the day:
> The darkness and the light are both alike to thee.
>   (vv.7-12)

David placed himself on God's side by stating in verses 19-22 that God's enemies were his enemies. He then made himself open before God when he wrote, "Search me, O God, and know my heart: try me, and know my thoughts: And see if there be any wicked way in me, and lead me in the way everlasting" (vv. 23-24).

Psalm 103 is a glorious paean of praise to God. The first verse, the last verse, and three verses in between open with the words "Bless the Lord." *Bless* is a stronger and more personal word than *praise*. David called for the heavenly hosts, earthly men, and even the inanimate world to glorify God.

In verses 1 and 2, he shows us how to praise God: (1) personally—no one else can do it for us; (2) spiritually—it must be from the soul and not simply outward show; (3) completely—"all that is is within me" and not lip service only; and (4) purposefully—lest we forget all His benefits.

In verses 3-19, David listed the benefits, or blessings, of the Lord. These verses are worth reading for

their sheer poetic beauty and the chance to meditate
on their implications. Particular favorites are these:

> He hath not dealt with us after our sins;
> nor rewarded us according to our iniquities.
> For as the heaven is high above the earth,
> so great is his mercy toward them that fear him.
> As far as the east is from the west,
> so far hath he removed our transgressions
>   from us. (vv.10-12)

ADONIJAH'S ABORTED COUP

David had lived a full though stressful life, so
that by the age of seventy his earthly body was "old
and stricken in years" (1 Kings 1:1). He became ill
and could not generate any warmth, even with
covers over him. With his father on his death bed
and his younger half-brother waiting to rule, Adonijah,
David's oldest living son, realized that if he wanted
to be king, the hour was at hand for him to assert
himself. He was a handsome man but had grown
up completely undisciplined, just like his older
brothers (1 Kings 1:6).

For his attempt to usurp the throne, Adonijah
gathered chariots and the usual fifty heralds to run
before him. (Appearance is always so important to
the insecure and the pretender.) Amazingly, the great
commander Joab and Abiathar, the priest of David
from the early outlaw days, gave their support to
Adonijah. The reason for their decision is not revealed.

Adonijah then invited his fellow princes (except
Solomon), the men of Judah, and others to attend
his "inauguration." While those attending were "eat-

ing and drinking with him and saying, 'Long live King Adonijah!' " (1 Kings 1:25, NIV), those members of the court favoring Solomon were busy at King David's bedchamber in the palace. Nathan the prophet had Bathsheba remind David of his oath that their son Solomon would follow him as king. She then told David of Adonijah's usurpation and of Joab and Abiathar's betrayal. She tried to rally the feeble king to action by saying, "The eyes of all Israel are upon thee, that thou shouldest tell them who shall sit on the throne of my lord the king after him" (1 Kings 1:20). As a personal touch, she reminded her husband of the dire things that would happen to both her and Solomon if he did not block Adonijah's evil action.

While Bathsheba was speaking to David, Nathan came in and confirmed her words. For one last glorious moment, the aged king became the decisive David of years past. He ordered Zadok (the high priest), Nathan, and Benaiah (the commander of the king's bodyguards), to put Solomon on his (David's) own mule, take him down to Gihon, and there anoint him king. Then they were to blow the trumpet and say, "Long live King Solomon!" Finally, they were to bring him back to the palace and put him on the throne (1 Kings 1:33-35).

The royal procession started out from the palace to a public part of the city, with Solomon riding on King David's personal mule, which would have been an offense punishable by death unless ordered by the king. The populace gathered from every side, and when Zadok poured the sacred oil on Solomon's head and pronounced him King Solomon, a trumpet of victory was blown, and an earth-shattering cheer went up from the crowd. The cheer was heard by

Adonijah's gathering, and it filled them with speculation until Jonathan, Abiathar's son, arrived with a
complete description of Solomon's coronation. The
guests around Adonijah melted away as ice melts
in July. Adonijah's dream melted away at the same
rate until, in fear of the new king, he fled for safety
(1 Kings 1:38-50).

DAVID'S LAST WORDS

The old monarch charged his teenage son who
was now seated on the throne of Israel,

> I am about to go the way of all the earth . . . So be
> strong, show yourself a man, and observe what the
> Lord your God requires: Walk in his ways, and keep
> his decrees and commands, his laws and require-
> ments, as written in the law of Moses, so that you
> may prosper in all you do and wherever you go, and
> that the Lord may keep his promise to me, "If your
> descendants watch how they live, and if they walk
> faithfully before me with all their heart and soul,
> you will never fail to have a man on the throne of
> Israel." (1 Kings 2:2-4, NIV)

What more could any man want from a son than
that he should prove himself to be a man pure and
holy on one side, and courageous on the other?
These were qualities that made David a great leader
and Jesus the greatest of all.

In these last words to Solomon, David referred to
the sure promise Jehovah had made to him, which
was that he would establish David's house as the
royal family and that through his house the promised
Messiah would come. This faithful hope and comfort

were expanded upon in David's last words as found in 2 Samuel 23:1-7.

There's something special about a person's last words. They often seem to give an exalted and detached, panoramic view of that person's disappointments and victories, fears and hopes, joys and sorrows. David prefaced his last words this way:

> The oracle of David son of Jesse,
>   the oracle of the man exalted by the Most High,
> the man anointed by the God of Jacob,
>   Israel's singer of songs. (v. 1, NIV)

David was satisfied that of his many achievements, he would be remembered largely as "Israel's singer of songs"—or, as the King James Version so beautifully translates it, "the sweet psalmist of Israel." He continued:

> The Spirit of the Lord spoke through me;
>   his word was on my tongue.
> The God of Israel spoke,
>   the Rock of Israel said to me:
> "When one rules over men in righteousness,
>   when he rules in the fear of God,
> he is like the light of morning at sunrise
>   on a cloudless morning,
> like the brightness after rain
>   that brings the grass from the earth" (vv. 2-4, NIV).

Without qualification, David stated that God spoke both to him and through him in describing the ultimate king, the Messiah.

Finally, in verses 5-7, David admitted he had not been the perfect ruler but rejoiced that God had made an everlasting covenant with him and that the perfect ruler, the Christ, would come through his family.

"So David slept with his fathers, and was buried in the city of David" (1 Kings 2:10). "He died in a good old age, full of days, riches, and honor" (1 Chron. 29:28). "David reigned over Israel . . . forty years: seven years reigned he in Hebron, and thirty three years reigned he in Jerusalem" (1 Kings 2:11).

David physically was taken from the scene, but his presence was to linger through the generations that followed. Every king was compared to him. Of Solomon it was said, "His heart was not perfect with the Lord his God, as was the heart of David his father" (1 Kings 11:4). Of his great grandson Abijah it was written, "His heart was not perfect with the Lord his God, as the heart of David his father" (1 Kings 15:3).

The Lord wrote David's epitaph: "David did that which was right in the eyes of the Lord, and turned not aside from any thing that he commanded him all the days of his life, save only in the matter of Uriah the Hittite" (1 Kings 15:5). In human memory, one evil deed done by an individual may eclipse a multitude of good deeds. But in God's memory, the good in a man's life takes precedence over the bad. How thankful we should be!

The light of God surrounded David, the power of God protected him, the love of God engulfed him, and the blessed presence of God watched over his every move.

CONCLUSION

In the introduction of David's life, Psalm 23 was

used to express David's personal relationship with Jehovah. In closing our study of his life, we will use the first psalm, which seems to have been his poetic charge to Solomon and to each of us. (The Bible does not ascribe this psalm to anyone, and Jerome said it might be called "the preface of the Holy Spirit" to the entire collection of psalms, but the phrasing is David's. A lifetime of experiencing the Lord as his shepherd is clearly heard in this psalm to the young people of a thousand generations.)

"Blessed is the man that walketh not in the counsel of the ungodly, nor standeth in the way of sinners, nor sitteth in the seat of the scornful" (v. 1). Walking, standing, and then sitting are the sequential steps to becoming involved in an evil life. A person is attracted toward sin by the counsel of promoters of wickedness; next, he stops and vicariously enjoys the pleasures of sin; and then he goes in and sits down at the Devil's table.

Blessed is he who does not follow the broad and downward way, but rather looks up and finds "his delight is in the law of the Lord; and in his law doth he meditate day and night" (v. 2). The person who follows this way is righteous, and "he shall be like a tree planted by the rivers of water, that bringeth forth his fruit in his season, his leaf also shall not wither; and whatsoever he doeth shall prosper" (v. 3).

Christians were called "trees of righteousness, the planting of the Lord, that he might be glorified" by Isaiah (Isa. 61:3) many centuries before the first disciple of Christ was called a Christian. There are so many likenesses between trees and Christians. They both have to be planted and then must grow and bear fruit. The Christian is planted with the seed of the Word of God entering his mind (Luke 8:11), and he grows in Christ to bear the fruit of the Spirit (Gal. 5:22). He is likened in Psalm 92:12-14 to a cedar in Lebanon that is ever green, and to a palm tree in the hot desert that never ceases to grow. If we are disciples of Christ, we will be ever active in the Lord's work, strive though we are in the world's materialistic desert, and never cease growing in both faith and wisdom. But "the ungodly are not so: but are like the chaff which the wind driveth away. Therefore the ungodly shall not stand in the judgment, nor sinners in the congregation of the righteous. For the Lord knoweth the way of the righteous: but the way of the ungodly shall perish" (vv. 4-6).

May we, like David, love the Lord and His Word and commit ourselves to walking with Him in His Way every day of our lives. May the Lord know your way.

Putting Truth into Action

1. The wise woman of Abel made a brutal agreement with Joab in order to protect her city. How can we settle disputes between friends, in families, or within nations in ways more consistent with Jesus' call to be peacemakers?

2. What lessons from the way David prepared Solomon and the leaders of Israel for Solomon's ascension can we apply to the training of our children or the preparation of someone to follow us in an assignment?

3. Amasa always seemed never to be at the right

place when needed. Discuss what one can do to overcome such a trait today.

4. What can we do today to make sure we are following God's pattern in life and worship?

5. What lesson from David's life can you begin to put into practice *today*?

FOOTNOTES

1. In Revelation 22:16, Jesus stated He was the "root," meaning the source, of David, and the "offspring," meaning the product, of David. Christ was both before and after David, and in David He was typified.
2. The book of Psalms is composed of five collections of psalms written over a 300-year period. The first collection was made by Solomon soon after David's death. This collection is called book one and is composed of forty-one psalms, thirty-seven of which are credited to David. Book two, Psalms 42-72, was collected soon after book one by Korahite Levites. Eighteen of the thirty-one psalms in book two are attributed to David. Book three is credited to King Hezekiah (2 Chron. 29:30) and is composed of only seventeen psalms (73-89). Only one of these (86) is David's. Book four, Psalms 90-106, was collected by Ezra and Nehemiah 600 years after David, during the last days of the Old Testament. Two psalms by David are included. The last book, book five, has a treasure chest of fifteen psalms by David among its forty-four. This collection was also gathered by Ezra and Nehemiah, according to Jewish sources. This five-part anthology contains psalms written by Moses, Solomon, and unnamed Jews as late as during the return from Babylonian captivity. At least seventy-three, almost half, of the psalms are attributed to David. The psalms are not arranged chronologically;

some of David's early poems are placed far after others written much later in his life. David's psalms were filled with metaphors and other figures of speech drawn from his shepherding days. His psalms, like his personality, are vigorous and straightforward. In reading his psalms, one must watch for the frequent sudden changes in mood or time; David was a volatile person, and his psalms reflect his thinking.

David's 85 Psalms

Psalms of early life: 18

7	13	23	52	57	104
11	17	34	54	59	109
12	22	35	56	63	142

Psalms of the period of his victorious reign: 22

2	16	20	27	60	101	107
8	18	21	29	68	105	110
15	19	24	36	96	106	118
						133

Psalms from his great sin through his flight from Absalom: 21

3	6	31	39	51	64	91
4	28	32	40	55	69	136
5	30	38	41	62	70	143

Psalms of his closing days: 4

1	37	103	139

Undated psalms of David: 20

9	25	58	86	122	138	144
10	26	61	108	124	140	145
14	53	65	114	131	141	

3. When Jesus' disciples could not cast out a demon, Jesus did. "Why?" they cried. Jesus answered, "Because of your unbelief: for verily I say unto you, If ye have faith as a grain of mustard seed . . . nothing shall be impossible unto you" (Matt. 17:14-20).

4. "For he did put his life in his hand" (1 Sam. 19:5). "As David in his youth, and on the threshold of his public career, overcame the strong enemy of Israel in single combat, so Jesus in youth, and on the threshold of his public life, encountered the adversary of the people of God, and overcame the tempter in the wilderness. Then as David endured much before he reached the throne, so Jesus Christ endured much before his father raised him up and gave him both glory and power. During the time of his lowly suffering Jesus was, like his ancestor David, solaced by love and pursued by envy" (D. Fraser, *The Pulpit Commentary*, vol. 4, pa. 356).

5. David's fight with the lion as a young shepherd made a deep impression on him. Not only did he tell Saul of the encounter to prove God's favor was with him, but seven times in his early psalms he also mentioned lions. His son Solomon had a great and costly throne made with twelve lions stationed symbolically on its six steps (1 Kings 10:18-20). Father Israel had previously used the lion to characterize the tribe of Judah as the ruling tribe (Gen. 49:8-10). Because of his great power, Jesus is called "the Lion of the tribe of Judah, the Root of David" (Rev. 5:5).

6. When the Israelite women sang the praises of David, as in 1 Samuel 18:7, they sang alternately; thus, they answered one another. This alternate singing style led to the psalms being composed in parallel sentences rather than in regular meter. And we, influenced by the Hebrew temple services that used the psalms, have inherited the method of chanting antiphonally (*The Pulpit Commentary*, vol. 4, pa. 340).

7. The enemies of Israel in David's time (see the map on page 14). About 150 years after the great flood, Jehovah

confused the one common language and thus divided
men into what would become three great families of
nations, which came from the three sons of Noah: Shem,
Ham, and Japheth (Gen. 10:32). The descendants of Ham,
through his son Canaan, migrated eastward and settled
in what was to be called "the promised land," or Canaan.
The general term *Canaanites* is often broken down into
tribal names: Amorites, Hittites, Jebusites, Havites, Periz-
zites, and Amalekites. These people were the nations
inhabiting the land Jehovah eventually gave to Israel, His
chosen people, in the days of Joshua.

The Israelites did not drive out all the Canaanites as
God had directed them to do, so God used those enemies,
saying, "Through them I may prove Israel, whether they
will keep the way of the Lord" (Judg. 2:22). The Canaanites were still very much in existence in David's
times. However, the chief enemy of Israel was Philistia,
peopled by the tribes of the five lords of the Philistines
(Judg. 3:3). They also descended from Ham but through
his son Mizraim, who originally settled in Egypt. The
Philistines were therefore not natives of the promised
land but migrants who had pushed northward along the
coast of the Mediterranean Sea. They were the ancestors
of the present-day Palestinians, many of whom remain
enemies of the Israelis.

Note that the Canaanite tribe of the Amorites is not to
be confused with the Ammonites, another enemy of Israel.
The Ammonites lived to the north of the Dead Sea and
west of the Jordan River. They were descendants of Lot,
the nephew of Abraham, through his younger daughter
(Gen. 19:30-38). To the south of the Ammonites lived the
Moabites, who also came from Lot. South of the land of
Moab and of the Dead Sea lived the Edomites, cousins
of the Israelites and their bitter enemies. They descended
from Esau, the brother of Jacob, the father of the twelve
tribes of Israel (Gen. 36:9).

CHAPTER 2

1. See 1 Samuel 16:14 and 18:10. "All must come from the Almighty, evil as well as good, inasmuch as all things are in his hand, and whatever is must be by his permission" (R. Payne Smith). Read also Job 1:8-12.

God freely gave of His Holy Spirit to Saul, but when He was rejected by Saul's freely committed sins, He withdrew His Holy Spirit. "It is a spiritual agency of God, which brings to bear upon Saul the dark and fiery powers of Divine wrath which he aroused by sin" (Delitzsch).

As the same rays of the sun that melt the ice also harden the clay, so the same gospel (word, spirit) of God becomes "to one an odor of death that leads to death, and to others an odor of life that leads to life" (2 Cor. 2:16, Weymouth).

The Word of God is a sharp, two-edged sword that may cut away the evil or the good in our lives depending on whether we choose to obey or disobey.

2. First Samuel 18:25 says Saul desired a hundred foreskins. First Samuel 18:27 says David gave him two hundred. The Septuagint says one hundred. Since in 2 Samuel 3:14 David says he espoused Michal for one hundred, this writer concludes the number 200 in 1 Samuel 18:27 is probably a copyist's error created at some point in the thousands of years of Old Testament transcription.

3. In Old Testament times, lying to protect life seems to have been considered justifiable.

We have already seen Michal lie to protect her husband (1 Sam. 19:17) and Jonathan lie for his friend (1 Sam. 20:28-29). We will also see lying practiced in 2 Samuel 17:20 to protect David's spies. A similar case was Rahab's, where she was blessed for lying (Josh. 2:1-21).

Furthermore, David was not the first of Christ's ancestors to practice deception. Abraham and Isaac both bent the truth to protect their lives rather than put their trust in God to deliver them (Gen. 12:10-20; 20:1-7; 26:6-9).

Feeling a need to lie to protect innocent life creates a great moral dilemma that is no easier to resolve today than it was in David's time.

4. Consider one line from verse 8 of Psalm 56 that reads, "Put thou my tears into thy bottle." David was requesting the Lord that his sorrowful trials not go unnoticed or be forgotten. In the heart of every compassionate parent are stored the tears of his children. How much more is this true in the heart of a compassionate God? It was in this line of thought that the prophet Jeremiah asked God to "remember my sorrows" and then wrote, "This I recall to my mind, therefore have I hope. It is of the Lord's mercies that we are not consumed, because his compassions fail not. They are new every morning. . . . The Lord is good . . . to the soul that seeketh him" (Lam. 3:21-25).

5. Psalm 34 has its Messianic foreshadowing in verses 19-20 where David says, "Many are the afflictions of the righteous; but the Lord delivereth him out of them all. He keepeth all his bones: not one of them is broken." In speaking of no bones being broken, David is looking both backward and forward; backward to the lamb sacrificed at the original Passover (Exod. 12:46), and forward to Christ, our sacrificial lamb (1 Cor. 5:7). The innocent blood of the pure unspotted lamb with not a bone broken protected the Israelites from the wrath of God that passed over the land of Egypt (Exod. 12). The pure innocent blood of Jesus can protect us from the everlasting wrath of God. John states in his record of Christ's crucifixion, "For these things were done, that the Scripture should be fulfilled, A bone of him shall not be broken" (John 19:36).

CHAPTER 3

1. The inspired author of Hebrews 2:12 quotes Psalms 22:22 verbatim with the exception of one word. The generic word "praise" is modified by the specific word

"sing." Is there significance in this change? Is any change made by the Holy Spirit insignificant? In the New Testament the music "in the church" is always singing, the beautiful music made upon the God-given harp of the human vocal chords.

2. "And every one that was in distress, and every one that was in debt, and everyone that was discontented, gathered themselves unto him; and he became a captain over them" (1 Sam. 22:2). David made them soldiers of the spear to establish and expand God's earthly kingdom. Jesus made his disciples soldiers of the cross to establish and expand God's earthly kingdom. Jesus made his disciples soldiers of the cross to establish and expand the spiritual kingdom of God.

Some of David's motley disciples became "mighty men" like the Knights of the Round Table of King Arthur. Some of Jesus' disciples became apostles who gathered around the Lord's Table.

3. The Lord gave Moses directions for making the sacred vestment for the high priest in Exodus 28 and 39. The ephod was a decorated vest to which was attached, with chains and rings of gold, the precious pouch, or breastplate, of judgment. "And thou shalt put in the breastplate of judgment the Urim and the Thumim; and they shall be upon Aaron's heart, when he goeth in before the Lord" (Exod. 28:30). The Urim (light) and Thumim (perfection) seem to have been two stones by which Jehovah answered questions and gave judgments for His people. How they operated when serving as God's oracle has produced much speculation by commentators.

After the massacre at Nob, Abiathar brought this holy ephod to David, who made frequent use of it to make inquiries of God. Following David's time, the ephod of judgment disappeared and was longed for in the days of the Jewish return from Babylonian captivity (Ezra 2:63). During that period, the prophet Hosea wrote that "after many days" without a king, sacrifices, or the ephod, there would come in the latter days "David, their king" with sacrifice and ephod. Thus, the ephod disappeared with King David and reappeared in a spiritual sense with Christ, the son of David. Christ answers all our questions to God. He is our Light and Perfection.

4. Because David asked God to "fight against them that fight against me" (v. 1) and to "let them be clothed with shame and dishonor" (v. 26), Psalm 35 is numbered among the "vindictive psalms" by some commentators. The proper meaning of vindictive is "that which proceeds from or shows a revengeful spirit." David showed the very opposite of a revengeful spirit in his dealings with Saul and others, however.

More properly, these psalms should be classified as "imprecatory psalms," because David called upon God to curse or cause certain calamities to fall upon his evil enemies. Imprecatory means "cursing."

These psalms cause great chagrin to certain commentators who try their best to rationalize them, because they are distressed that any righteous person would pray for calamities to come upon the wicked. When they get to Psalm 109, they faint, because there David called for God to curse his enemies, saying: "Let his days be few"; "Let his children be fatherless"; "Let his wife be a widow": "Let his posterity be cut off."

Theological writer J. Hammond attempts to neutralize this psalm by telling us these curses were not spoken by David but by Shimei about David. The text is too clear, however, for such dishonest manipulation. We must simply accept the fact that David was a warrior with strong human feelings who, at that time, was being heavily "leaned upon." Since the Lord uttered not one word of condemnation of David's imprecatory prayers, neither will this writer.

There are several truths we must bear in mind when reading these psalms: (1) Mr. C. Clemance, in *The Pulpit Commentary*, has well stated that the psalms are not the words of God to man but the words of man to God. No man is perfect in his words and deeds or else there would be no need for the sacrifice of our Savior. (2) David had the perfect right, as a child of God, to pour out his heart without reservation to Him. Is it not the desire of the understanding parent that his children feel free to express their innermost thoughts? This allows the parent the opportunity to guide his children to a more perfect knowledge of God's will. No man can pray beyond the level of his own spiritual growth. If, in placing our cares and wishes before God, we say anything amiss, God will forgive what is wrong and answer us in His own proper way. "The Spirit also helpeth our infirmities: for we know not what we should pray for as we ought: but the Spi(rit itself maketh intercession for us with groanings which cannot be uttered" (Rom. 8:26).

(3) David clearly felt his course was righteous and thus identified his enemies as God's enemies. He passionately prayed for their defeat and yearned for God's vindication of the right. He knew vengeance and recompense belong to the Lord who had said, "Their foot shall slide in due time" for the day of their calamity is at hand" (Deut. 32:35: Rom. 12:19). (4) Jesus clearly separated the person from his evil deeds and taught us to love our enemies and pray for their salvation. On the other hand, Christ taught us to hate their evil works (Rev. 2:6). God-fearing people today sympathize with the spirit of David's imprecatory psalms and yearn to see the righteous triumph and the evil destroyed. Today, for example, we shouldn't pray for a plague to come upon those who flagrantly abuse their God-given sexuality, but we may pray that acts of perversion cease from the face of the earth. How God answers the prayer is completely His to decide.

Vengeance and punishment are parts of the doctrine of the Old and New Testaments just as much as love and forgiveness. ". . . when the Lord Jesus shall be revealed from heaven with his mighty angels, in flaming fire taking vengeance on them that know not God, and that obey not the gospel of our Lord Jesus Christ: who shall be punished with everlasting destruction from the presence of the Lord" (2 Thess. 1:7-9).

5. The same Hebrew word used for "bundle" in 1 Samuel 25:29 is used in Genesis 42:35, where it is written, "every man's bundle of money." Men in Old Testament times carried their valuables in a wallet, or bundle, even as we carry valuables in a wallet.

Abigail told David he was a part of Jehovah's "bundle of life," one of His most precious possessions. If we today are among the few (Matt. 7:14; 22:14), we may know, as David did, that we are part of Jehovah's "bundle of life." "They shall be mine, saith the Lord of hosts, in that day when I make up my jewels" (Mal. 3:17).

The two Hebrew words translated "in the bundle of life" form a common inscription on Jewish gravestones, because the Talmud interprets them to mean "saved for a future life."

6. "I have sinned" are three difficult words to say if one realizes the hideousness of sin and is truly filled with sorrow for what he has done. But these words slip easily from the tongue of one who feels lightly the guilt of sin and has not truly repented. This was true with Saul. Saul had said these words before to Samuel and to David but had not shown "fruits worthy of repentance" (Luke 3:8). We cannot judge a man when he says, "I have sinned." God knows the innermost thoughts of our hearts and so can judge. The apostle John, writing to Christians, gave this great comfort: "If we confess our sins, he is faithful and just to forgive us our sins, and to cleanse us from all unrighteousness" (1 John 1:9).

David, much later in life, would also say, "I have sinned," but he would water his couch with the tears of repentance.

CHAPTER 4

1. The moon and artificial satellites that orbit the earth

follow an elliptic path, with the perigee being the closest point to the earth and the apogee being the farthest point.

David centered his life on Jehovah, but sometimes the influence of God upon his life was greater than at other times. Christians orbit around Christ, and we should not be surprised to find that our relationship with Christ is not always the same. The important thing is knowing what to do when we find we are moving away from Christ. We are moving away when reading the Bible daily becomes a chore, when the minister's sermons seem dry and windy, when pessimistic thoughts of "What's the use?" fill our minds, or when we sing the Lord's praise with a yawn. Then it is time to fire our correcting rockets and draw closer to the Savior.

What are these life-correcting rockets? They are prayer and more prayer, involvement in good works, reading the gospel of John or Peter's two epistles, meditating on eternity, talking to a fellow Christian. These are boosters that can turn our direction back toward Christ and a fulfilling life.

2. God has given us by inspired revelation what we need to know about the future so our actions may be guided correctly as we live in the present (2 Pet. 1:3; 2 Tim. 3:16). But that which He revealed not, "the secret things belong unto the Lord our God: but those things which are revealed belong unto us and to our children for ever" (Deut. 29:29). Thus, to seek to know the secret things has always been condemned in the Bible. In the New Testament we have the example of the apostle Paul's casting out a foretelling spirit from a maid in Philippi (Acts 16:16-18). Read also Isaiah 8:19, Deuteronomy 18:9-14, and Leviticus 19:31.

Astrology, necromancy, and other efforts at occult divination are condemned. If there is any validity to any of these efforts, it is derived from the power of the Devil (2 Thess. 2:8-12).

3. The book of Jasher appears to have been a collection of patriotic ballads about Hebrew heroes and battles that

was taught to Jewish children to instill a sense of pride in their heritage. Our American history books were used in a similar way before they were stripped of real heroes by secular humanists who have also attempted to remove all the supernatural miracles from the Bible.

Another reference to it is found in Joshua 10:13 concerning the crucial battle for the promised land during which God prolonged the day by causing the sun to stand still. The book has been lost for ages.

CHAPTER 5

1. The first verse of Psalm 27 reads, "The Lord is my light." David alone, of all the Old Testament authors, made this statement that's so much a part of New Testament doctrine. "I am the light of the world: he that followeth me shall not walk in darkness, but shall have the light of life," Jesus said in John 8:12.

2. In Psalm 27:13 is an aposiopesis. That is not a strange disease; in rhetoric, it is a sudden interruption of thought in the middle of a sentence, as if the speaker were unwilling or unable to continue.

Notice that translators have supplied the words "would have fainted" or similar words to verse 13 to complete David's thought. It is far more dramatic if the verse is left alone to read, as it did in the original, "If I had not believed that I would see the goodness of Jehovah in this life I _____."

3. The Hebrew word *Baal* originally meant "lord" or "master" and was applied to many local deities. It wasn't until the time of King Ahab, about 910 B.C. (1 Kings 16), that Baal became a term of reproach. Ahab and his evil wife, Jezebel, attempted to replace the worship of Jehovah with the worship of the Phoenician idol, Baal. After that time, the term *Bosheth*, meaning "the shame," was substituted for Baal in older names of which it had formed a part. Therefore, Esh-baal, or Ish-baal, which meant "man

of the lord" or "lordly man," was changed to Ish-bosheth, or "man of shame."

Jonathan's son was named Merib-baal, or "the lord's strife" (1 Chron. 8:34), but the scribe who later wrote the inspired account changed it to Mephibosheth, or "shameful strife."

4. For an Israelite to say "from Dan to Beer-sheba" is like an American's saying "from Maine to California." It means from the village of Dan, located in the extreme north of the promised land, to Beer-sheba, located in the extreme south.

5. There are some things that are good but not pleasant, and there are some things that are pleasant but not good, but the oneness of mind that maintains unity and peace among brethren is both good and pleasant. In that tender prayer recorded for us in John 17, Christ prayed that his followers might be one even as He and the Father are one. Following that example, Paul wrote of the oneness we have together in the Lord in Ephesians 4:3-5 and rebuked those who cause division in 1 Corinthians 1.

6. It seems certain that David was guided by a will far higher than his own, because God had promised through Moses, in Deuteronomy 12:1-5, that "in the land, which the Lord . . . giveth thee to possess it. . . . your God shall choose [a site] out of all your tribes to put his name there." His habitation would be there, and there His people were to make their sacrifices. Again in 2 Chronicles 6:6 Jehovah said, "I have chosen Jerusalem, that my name might be there."

7. "We're marching to Zion, beautiful, beautiful Zion,

We're marching upward to Zion, the beautiful city of God." We sing these words written by Isaac Watts and feel the pull toward that perfect city of the redeemed. The first use of the word *Zion* in the Bible is found in 2 Samuel 5:7. It was popularized as God's special acre by both David and Isaiah. However, it was seldom used by the inspired authors of the last period of the Old Testament and is found only six times in the New Testament.

Yet it remains the symbol of the holiest part of the holy city of Jerusalem to believers.

A number of scholars have tried to determine the original meaning of the word *Zion*, but none have succeeded with any certainty.

8. "David perceived that the Lord had established him king over Israel, and that he had exalted his kingdom for his people Israel's sake" (2 Sam. 5:12). David's wisdom, humility, gratitude, and unselfishness are shown in this perception. David's divine son, Jesus, also exalted not Himself but glorified His Father in heaven. He did not live or die for Himself but for us, God's chosen people, that we might be blessed. Even as Israel was blessed through God's use of David, so all nations are blessed through Christ, in fulfillment of the promise given Abraham so long ago in Genesis 18:18.

CHAPTER 6

1. When God delivered His people from Egyptian bondage, He gave Moses directions for building the tabernacle and its furnishings. It was a movable tent, pitched at the center of every encampment of the twelve tribes. Their place of worship and the heart of their religion, it was divided into the holy place and the most holy place, which was a perfect cube. In the midst of the most holy place rested an open-topped chest, or ark, completely overlaid with pure gold. It was twenty-seven inches deep, and forty-five inches long. In it were placed the two tablets of stone upon which the ten commandments were engraved, the rod of Aaron that budded, and an urn of manna (Heb. 9:4). Thus, the law, the authority, and the care of Jehovah for His people were symbolized by the items in the chest.

The Ark was covered by a lid of pure gold, with a cherubim standing with outstretched wings at each end.

This was the mercy seat where the presence of Jehovah could be found. God said, "There I will ... commune with thee from above the mercy seat, from between the two cherubims which are upon the ark of the testimony" (Exod. 25:22). It was, then, the one place where the localized presence of Jehovah could be found.

The Ark went ahead of the Israelites through the wilderness, across the swollen Jordan River, and into the promised land. It was Israel's "home base" until it was captured by the Philistines. Read 1 Samuel 4:1–7:2.

2. The Targums were like our commentaries on portions of the Bible today. By the time of the Babylonian captivity, the Jews had largely ceased to understand the language in which the older Scriptures were originally written. Thus, the Targums were explanations of these Scriptures, written in the Chaldic language for the benefit of the Jews of that day. A possible biblical reference to the Targums is found in Nehemiah 8:8.

3. At the close of this beautiful psalm of praise, "all the people said, Amen, and praised the Lord" (1 Chron. 16:36). The word *amen* means "so be it" or "let it be so." It is the scriptural word used to signify that we agree with the words of another, and it expresses our wish for the accomplishment of the praises and petitions made. It is found in both the Old and New Testaments. Its use in early Christian congregations was noted by Justin Martyr in A.D. 138, and by Dionysius of Alexander in A.D. 232. Jerome, in A.D. 331, spoke of the thundering sound of the "amen" of the Roman congregations.

4. The fine linen robes worn in God's service by the priests and Levites (1 Chron. 15:27) were a foreshadowing of the spiritual robes of good works to be worn by Christians (see Rev. 19:8).

5. Jesus Christ is called "the Lord of lords, and King of kings" in Revelation 17:1-4 and 19:16. He who was "the brightness of God's glory, and the express image of his person" (Heb. 1:3) was the fulfillment of the symbols of the Ark of God. He was and is the law, the mercy, and

the providential care of our God in one person. When He ascended into heaven and "sat down on the right hand of the Majesty on high" (Heb. 1:3), the gates of heaven opened wide and the jubilation far exceeded that which occurred when David brought the Ark through the gates of Jerusalem.

CHAPTER 7

1. David was the last individual in the Old Testament to receive from God the promise that the Savior of all mankind would come through him. The promise was first made to Abraham in Genesis 12:3. It was then made to Abraham's son Isaac in Genesis 26:4, and to his grandson Jacob in Genesis 28:14. Thus, the three great patriarchs of Israel received the promise. Furthermore, the tribe of Judah was singled out in Genesis 49:10. Finally, of the families making up the tribe of Judah, David's family was selected to provide the Christ (2 Sam. 7:8-29 and 1 Chron. 17:4-15).

It's interesting to note that in Matthew's genealogy, Jesus came through Solomon, the son of David (Matt. 1:6), whereas in Luke's account Jesus came through Nathan, the son of David (Luke 3:31). Adam Clarke, H. Leo Boles, and many other Bible scholars believe Matthew gave the lineage of Jesus through Joseph, the adoptive father, whereas Luke gave the lineage through Mary, the mother of Jesus.

2. Jehovah God gave David a holy and sure promise and granted him a glimpse of the glorious future and divine mercy in the substance of the gospel of Christ. The doctrine of the resurrection and of victory over the grave had been hoped for and hinted at earlier, but it was revealed to David. He vicariously shouted it out in Psalm 16:10: "For thou wilt not leave my soul in hell; neither wilt thou suffer thine Holy One to see corruption." He whispered it in 2 Samuel 12:23 for all who have lost a loved one: "Now he is dead, wherefore should I fast? can I bring him back again? I shall go to him, but he shall

not return to me." Christ is "the firstfruits of them that slept" and then "they that are Christ's" (1 Cor. 15:20-23). First through his death we are given new life in Him (Rom. 6:4), and then we shall be raised to reign with Him forever.

We can see clearly how important it is to understand the Old Testament, because in it God laid the foundation for the New. Christ is in the Old in promise and in the New in fulfillment.

3. In Psalm 20:1, David has the people call upon "the God of Jacob" to set him on high. In no less than fifteen of his psalms, David wrote of the God who promised Jacob He would keep him wherever he went and bring him back to the promised land (Gen. 28:15). David associated himself with Jacob for good reason. Jacob had been an exile from his homeland to escape the wrath of Esau, even as David had been an exile from his homeland to escape Saul's wrath. In the future, Christ would be an exile in Egypt to escape the wrath of Herod. God brought them all back. Further, Jacob, whose name meant "supplanter," had supplanted Esau in the lineage leading to the Messiah, and David had supplanted Saul as the king of God's chosen people. Jesus also supplanted the old covenant with a better one (Heb. 8:6-7).

4. 1 Samuel 17 says David killed Goliath, but 2 Samuel 21:19 states that Elhanan, one of David's "mighty men," slew Goliath. The parallel passage 1 Chronicles 20:5, says that Elhanan killed Lahmi, the brother of Goliath.

There has been much written on these passages but little accord. It appears that there was a giant who had four sons who were all large. All these giants were slain by David and his warriors. Their individual names are not clearly distinguishable. One of them had six toes on each foot and six fingers on each hand.

196

A possible accounting of this unusual family and their fate is:

Giant	Killed by
Goliath, the father	David
Ishbi-Benob	Abishai, 25 or more years later
Saph or Sippai	Sibbecai
Lahmi, brother or son of Goliath	Elhanan
(The one with 24 digits)	Jonathan, David's nephew

CHAPTER 8

1. We become so involved with the rich man and the poor man that we forget there is a third character in the parable, the one who precipitated the evil action. Jewish scholars did not ignore him. "They said the traveler represents that which they call 'the evil disposition,' or desire that is in us, which must be diligently watched and observed when we feel its motions. In the beginning it is but a traveler, but in time it becomes a guest, and in the end is the master of the house" (Patrick).

In Job 1:7, Satan is pictured as a traveler "going to and fro in the earth, and ... walking up and down in it." The Devil is a skilled master at knowing a person's weakness and placing a temptation before him at his most susceptible time. Satan entered David's mind when he saw Bathsheba from the rooftop. David entertained Satan by committing adultery with Uriah's one wife while he himself had many willing wives and concubines.

We must be on guard at all times against the evil traveler, for we know two things: the Devil is like a roaring lion, seeking whom he may devour (1 Pet. 5:8), but if we resist him, he will flee from us (James 4:7).

2. The dictionary defines despise as meaning "to regard as contemptible or worthless, to scorn and to look down upon." A person may deny that he considers the holy

Word of God to be worthless, but when he transgresses clearly stated biblical commands, his actions speak louder than his words. Jesus said, "Not every one that sayeth unto me, Lord, Lord, shall enter into the kingdom of heaven; but he that doeth the will of my Father which is in heaven" (Matt. 7:21).

3. The story is told of a young man on a high school baseball team. He had committed an error, and the coach lectured him severely and sent him over to stand with the third-string team. The well-disciplined boy complained to a friend, "Coach is always picking on me." The friend replied, "Consider yourself lucky. If the coach ever quits talking to you, it means he's given up on you."

God quit talking to Saul because there was no hope of his changing, but He corrected David because He could see the potential for good. We read in Proverbs 3:11-12, "My son, do not despise the Lord's discipline and do not resent his rebuke because the Lord disciplines those he loves, as a father the son he delights in" (NIV).

4. In the fifth verse of Psalm 51, David wrote, "Behold, I was brought forth in iniquity; and in sin did my mother conceive me." This verse has given great comfort to those who believe in the doctrine that babies are born in a sinful and lost condition and need baptism as infants so that they may receive God's grace and be saved. Some paraphrases of the Bible reword this verse to clearly teach this despicable doctrine. An example from the Living Bible reads, "But I was born a sinner, yes, from the moment my mother conceived me." In order to show the error made by paraphrasing the fifth verse like that, let's substitute other nouns for *sin* and *iniquity* so that the verse reads as follows: "Behold I was brought forth in a watermelon field, and in a melon patch did my mother conceive me." The Living Bible paraphrase would then read, "But I was born a watermelon, yes, from the moment my mother conceived me." Hopefully, the error of the paraphrase is obvious.

198

Under what moral or spiritual conditions a woman conceives a child does not change the moral or spiritual condition of that baby. The moral or spiritual conditions of the parents when the baby is born does not affect the moral or spiritual nature of the child. Christ clearly teaches that children are both pure and holy in Matthew 18:1-6, Mark 10:13-16; and Luke 18:15-17. We must become as little children in our relationship to God; safe, not lost. For a supporting passage in the Old Testament, read Ezekiel 18.

It was noted early in this book that we know nothing of David's mother. It is possible that from this verse (Psalm 51:5) we learn more of the moral character of David's mother than from any other passage.

5. Some may wonder why years of suffering followed David's great sin if God had forgiven him. We must see the vast difference between the removal of guilt and the consequences of sin. Not recognizing this difference has led to the misunderstanding of the "original" sin of Adam and Eve. We still suffer from the consequences of their sin as stated in Genesis 3:14-19, but we don't bear the guilt of their sin. Forgiveness of sin takes place in the mind of God and changes the personal relationship between God and the sinful person. The individual forgiven is (1) released from the condemnation brought by sin, (2) restored to God's grace, and (3) enjoys a renewal of the heart in righteousness. Cancellation of the earthly *consequences* of sin, however, is not a part of forgiveness. A boy might be forgiven by the owner of an apple orchard for stealing some of his apples, but this forgiving action would not cure the stomachache that was the consequence of eating green apples.

CHAPTER 9

1. We cannot help but note how often alcohol was included in wicked plots. Absalom waited until alcohol

had clouded the mind of Amnon before he struck. David had thought alcohol would dull the resolve of Uriah and bring to the front his more fleshly desires. Alcohol is a favorite tool of the Devil.

2. Mules may seem an odd choice for royal transportation, since the ass had been used for riding prior to this time. This is the first mention of the mule, but we find that David had a favorite mule (1 Kings 1:33), and Solomon received mules as tribute (1 Kings 10:25). Israelites were forbidden to breed hybrids (Lev. 19:19); thus, all mules were probably secured by tribute or trade from other nations. Horses seem to have been used chiefly to pull chariots (*The Pulpit Commentary*).

3. The wise woman of Tekoah said she didn't want her last son killed because it would "quench my coal" and leave no one to perpetuate the family name (2 Sam. 14:7).

In those days and for many years thereafter, caring for and protecting a source of fire was a very important responsibility, because methods of starting fire for light, cooking, and heat were not readily available. It was natural, then, that the tradition of passing on the family's literal coal of fire be applied to the passing on of the family's name. This concept was enhanced by the ritual of passing on the sacred fire of God's altar (Lev. 6:12-13).

4. "But God does not take away life; instead, he devises ways so that a banished person may not remain estranged from him" (2 Sam. 14:14, NIV).

The wise woman of Tekoah, either in her wisdom or in her ignorance, correctly stated the relationship of Jehovah with mankind. In his grace toward man, God established a way to meet the demands of justice while allowing the lost to find their way back to him. Since the established penalty for sin was death, both physically and spiritually (Gen. 3:3, Ezek. 18:4), God devised the Gospel wherein the demands of justice are met by God's son dying in man's place which then gives man the opportunity of a new life in God.

200

Isn't it marvelous to find the Gospel of Christ prestated a thousand years before he lived on earth?

CHAPTER 10

1. Jesus Christ, like David, climbed the Mount of Olives with His heart breaking. He had told His apostles at the Last Supper of His impending betrayal by one of them and of Peter's three denials. On the mount in the garden of Gethsemane, he said to Peter, James, and John, "My soul is exceeding sorrowful, even unto death: tarry ye here, and watch with me. And he went a little further, and fell on his face, and prayed, saying, O my Father, if it be possible, let this cup pass from me: nevertheless, not as I will, but as thou wilt" (Matt. 26:38-39). He resigned His fate to God, even as His physical forefather had done.

CHAPTER 11

1. David wished he had been able to die for his son, wayward though the son had been. God our Father did die for us through His Son, Jesus. "For God so loved the world, that he gave his only begotten Son, that whosoever believeth in him should not perish, but have everlasting life" (John 3:16).

The heart-wringing words of David foreshadowed the words Jesus uttered for a wayward and rebellious people when He cried, "O Jerusalem, Jerusalem, thou that killest the prophets, and stonest them which are sent unto thee, how often would I have gathered thy children together, even as a hen gathereth her chickens under her wings, and ye would not!" (Matt. 23:37).

2. Today there are many who cannot understand why God takes no pleasure in the death of the wicked (Ezek. 18:32; 33:11), or why He doesn't simply destroy the Devil

and all his followers and thus instantly purify the world of all injustice, disease, and sorrow. What they don't understand is that the Lord "is long-suffering to us-ward, not willing that any should perish, but that all should come to repentance" (2 Pet. 3:9). God, like David, is a compassionate Father even to His rebellious children. But His Word teaches that at His set time, His patience will end and He will act decisively in separating the saved from the eternally lost.

3. When Jesus cleansed the temple of those misusing it, "His disciples remembered that it was written, 'The zeal of thine house hath eaten me up' " (John 2:17, from Psa. 69:9). Both David and Jesus had a much clearer view of God's plans for a pure and united house, or kingdom, than did the average son of Abraham, and their zeal to promote God's plan caused them to be at odds with their own people.

CHAPTER 12

1. David laid up untold riches of gold, silver, and jewels for the temple to be built in Jerusalem (1 Chron. 29:2-5), and Christ laid up unsearchable riches for the church that was to be first established in Jerusalem (Eph. 3:8).

David made all the necessary preparations for the establishment of the temple and then turned the actual construction over to Solomon. Even so, Jesus made all the necessary preparations for the building of the church and then turned the keys, or actual establishment, over to Peter and the apostles (Matt. 16:13-19, Acts 1-2).

David wanted a magnificent temple that would bring glory to Jehovah throughout all countries. Jesus desires a "glorious church, not having spot, or wrinkle, or any such thing; but that it should be holy and without blemish" (Eph. 5:27), bringing glory to God.

2. You may remember that the people of God were asked by Moses for a freewill offering of things precious to them

for the construction of the tabernacle in the wilderness (Exod. 35:4-9). Here we find David asking for such an offering for the building of the temple. Both temple and tabernacle were shadows of the church of Christ. In the building of the church, God made a freewill offering by giving His only begotten Son to die on the cross so that the spiritual temple of eternal salvation might become a reality. Devoting our lives to Jesus so that His church might fill the earth with His glory and grace is our freewill offering.

3. If, as the inspired David wrote, we exist in the mind of God even before our bodily parts develop in our mother's womb, then to willfully terminate that life before birth is as much murder as it is to terminate life *after* birth. In the eyes of God, birth is but a dramatic experience in the continuum of human life.